A Couple's Devotional

BRIDGING THE Gap

DANA FULLER

Studio Griffin
A Publishing Company
www.studiogriffin.net

Bridging the Gap: A Couple's Devotional. Copyright © 2020 Dana Fuller

All Rights Reserved. Printed in the United States of America.

No part of this book may be used or reproduced in any manner whatsoever without written permission except in the case of brief quotations embodied in critical articles and reviews.

For information, contact:
Studio Griffin
A Publishing Company
Garner, North Carolina
studiogriffin@outlook.com
www.studiogriffin.net

Cover Design by Ruth E. Griffin
Image by © Andrew Jackson

Scripture quotations marked KJV taken from The Holy Bible, King James Version. New York: American Bible Society: 1999.

Scripture quotations marked NKJV taken from New King James Version Second Edition. Copyright © 1995, 2006 by Thomas Nelson, Inc.

Scripture quotations marked AMP taken from The Amplified Bible, Copyright 1954, 1958, 1962, 1964, 1965, 1987, by the Lockman Foundation. All rights reserved. Used by permission.

Scripture quotations marked NIV taken from the Holy Bible, New International Version®. Copyright © 1973, 1978, 1984 International Bible Society. Used by permission of Zondervan. All rights reserved. The "NIV" and "New International Version" trademarks are registered in the United States Patent and Trademark Office by International Bible Society. Use of either trademark requires the permission of International Bible Society.

Scripture quotations marked MSG taken from Holy Bible: The Message (the Bible in contemporary language). 2005. Colorado Springs, CO: NavPress.

First Edition

ISBN-13: 978-1-7351353-2-8

Library of Congress Control Number: 2020913288

1 2 3 4 5 6 7 8 9 10

In loving memory of my mother, Floretha Davis Mack.
Your grace left fingerprints on our lives.
You will never be forgotten in our hearts.

TABLE OF CONTENTS

Foreword	1
Preface	3
Weeks 1-4: Your Garden	7
How Green Is Your Grass?	9
How to Cultivate Your Grass	12
Is The Grass Really Greener On The Other Side?	15
It's Time to Take Your Yard Back!	18
Weeks 5-9: Transformation	21
Metamorphosis Encounter	23
Empowered to Change Your Marriage	26
It's Time to Change	29
You Can Change	32
A Marriage Worth Fighting For	35
Weeks 10-15: Marriage	39
Are You Ready To Say, "I Do?"	41
Questions to Ask Before (And After) Marriage	44
Covenant Versus a Contract	47
We're Married, Now What? Making Time for Each Other	50
What Makes a Solid Foundation?	54
Thank You God for Our Marriage	57
Weeks 16-20: It's Worth the Work	59
Is It Time to Shift Gears?	61
Shifting Out of Park	64
Gears Are Like the Season	67
If It's Broken, Fix It	70
Don't Settle	74
Weeks 21-26: Listen: To God, to Your Marriage, and to Each Other	79
Frequency	81
God Can Put It Back Together	84
Bigger, Better, and Stronger	87
Falling in Love?	90
Follow the Directions	93
What Are You Hearing?	97

- Weeks 27-30: Your Marriage Toolbox 101
  - What's In Your Toolbox? 103
  - What's In Your Tool Box? (Communication) 106
  - What's In Your Tool Box? (Love) 109
  - What's In Your Toolbox? (Forgiveness) 112
- Weeks 31-35: Teamwork 115
  - Fostering Teamwork in Your Marriage 117
  - Tune-Up Your Marriage 120
  - Your Spouse is a Gift 123
  - Insulating Your Marriage 126
  - A Total Workout 129
- Weeks 36-39: Love 133
  - Romance in a Marriage 135
  - Keeping Your Love Alive 138
  - Make Every Day Valentine's Day! 141
  - The Perfect Marriage 144
- Weeks 40-43: Overcoming Temptation 147
  - Fighting Temptation 149
  - Temptation 101 152
  - Overcoming Temptation 155
  - Defining Temptation 158
- Weeks 44-48: Reviewing Dr. Chapman's Love Languages 161
  - Love Language #1: Words of Affirmation 163
  - Love Language #2: Quality Time 166
  - Love Language #3: Gifts 169
  - Love Language #4: Acts of Service 172
  - Love Language #5: Physical Touch 175
- Weeks 49-52: Common Challenges 179
  - Premature Ejaculation 181
  - Where Are The Fathers? 185
  - Oh, the In-Laws! 188
  - Empty Nest Syndrome 191
- A Final Thought 195
- Acknowledgments 197
- About the Author 199

A Couple's Devotional

BRIDGING THE
Gap

FOREWORD

What do you have when two creations, two worlds, two points of view or two souls attempt to occupy the same space? Some may say, "You have chaos." Others may say, "A stalemate or standoff." If we told you there is a way by which two can become one, would you look into it? If you said yes, well don't let go of this book. My wife, Angela, and I believe people should invest in their lives spiritually physically, financially, mentally, emotionally, and matrimonially. We are convinced this is necessary for those "two" to come together in harmony. Many couples want this but are frustrated, because of not properly perceiving the territory called Marriage.

Chauncy and Dana have poured their lives and hearts into this book. We've been covenant friends for over thirty years and they are called to help couples who are engaged, married, and/or thinking about marriage, navigate through the terrain of relationships. This book was birthed out of their personal journey and the Lord's guidance. We are honored to know them and be a part of this amazing undertaking.

We pray you invest in yourself and your spouse and make this book part of your library of spiritual self-care and matrimony. As you begin this devotional, you will discover how to take the necessary steps in "Bridging the Gap."

Tony and Angela Peterson

Senior Pastors and Founders
Every Walk of Life Ministries

Dana Fuller

PREFACE

Staying connected in a relationship sounds easy. At first, the couple feels invincible, as though their love can conquer the world. As time passes though, if the two fail to continue to place each other as a priority in the relationship, complacency will set in. If both parties do not take the necessary steps in "bridging the gap" when breaks appear, over time they can begin to detach, and separation will take over.

My husband, Chauncy, and I experienced "the disconnect" in our relationship. It happened at different times, in different seasons and in numerous areas: emotionally, mentally, financially, and sexually. However, by applying the Word of God and staying committed to each other, we were able to reconnect. We began by reading "God's Little Devotion book for Couples" the first few years of our marriage. We still had our issues, but we were able to get through them. Then during year seven, our relationship took a different route. We understood adjustments had to take place in both of us, so we started reading various Christian books, like Stormie Omartian's "The Power of a Praying Wife" and "The Power of a Praying Husband." It wasn't until we read "The Five Love Languages" by Gary Chapman though that we realized we were not communicating the love language that each of us needed to build our marriage. This revelation set in motion the steps to repairing some areas and strengthening others as we worked on reconnecting with each other. We understood that "bridging the gap" in our relationship was vital for the success of our marriage and each other, we understood we needed a tune-up. Isn't it amazing that we will sit for two to four hours while our car is being tuned-up, but we won't give our marriage the same consideration? If you want your marriage to be a marriage according to God's design, maybe it's time for a tune-up.

How to Use This Book

Every married person at one time or another has desired to experience a positive change in their marriage. If you haven't, keep on living, because you will. Now if your marriage is perfect and you've never needed to change in any areas of your relationship, then stop reading now—I'm not talking to you. I'm talking to people who are desperate for change, healing, and restoration in their marriage; people who are yearning to know God's plan and purpose for their marriage; people who are tired of the enemy sowing havoc in their relationship. **The Bible says the thief (Satan) comes to steal, kill, and destroy (John 10:10).**

I know plenty of people who are married, but are unhappy, lonely, and miserable. Is this God's design for marriage? Certainly not! God never intended for us to live under the same roof, to sleep in separate bedrooms or stay married just to avoid divorce. God always intended for marriages to be filled to abundance until it overflowed; if your marriage isn't, then there may be something within you that you need to change. Don't become the couple who awakens twenty years into their marriage and realizes that nothing in their relationship has changed. You have to speak life into your marriage with power and authority. We have the power within us, now it's time to use it. Otherwise, knowledge is puffed up if there is no application.

In the bestselling book, "The Five Love Languages," Dr. Gary Chapman states the reason many couples struggle is because they are speaking different love languages. If your native language is English, and you don't speak a foreign language, it would be quite difficult for you to communicate to another person who only speaks French. How ridiculous does that sound? Your language would be just as foreign to the other person as theirs is to you! Well, that's how my husband and I were for many years: we felt as if we were from two different planets. We sincerely believed we were communicating love to the other, but we had absolutely no idea why we weren't connecting.

During the first nine years of our marriage, my husband worked the night shift. Almost every Friday after he'd gotten some sleep, he would clean the entire apartment. This was an Act of Kindness, one of the love languages that Dr. Chapman identified in his book. This act of kindness continued even when we moved into our first home. And not just that: whenever he received a bonus check or extra cash, Chauncy would plan for us to go away on weekend excursions. He would handle all of the arrangements; all I had to do was pack the bags. These were my husband's ways of communicating his love to me; and while these acts of kindness were wonderful, however; this was his love language, not mine. **My love languages were Words of Affirmation, Quality Time, and Physical Touch. I showed my love to Chauncy by sending him love notes, by holding his hands privately and in public. I also enjoyed going on quiet walks in the park.**

Through Dr. Chapman's book, we discovered each other's love language, which enabled us to communicate and experience love according to God's master design. As a result, **we were inspired and realized our purpose was to share our experiences with others.** Along with my husband, I've written this book as part devotional, part testimony of our marriage in progress, in hopes that our experiences and transparency will help couples experience a marriage by God's design. We encourage you to read weekly, and to take advantage of the reflection page to write down your thoughts as you reflect on the devotional for the week.

Dana Fuller

Dana Fuller

Bridging The Gap

Weeks 1-4
YOUR GARDEN

Dana Fuller

∽ WEEK 1 ∽

How Green Is Your Grass?
I have come that they may have life and
that they may have it more abundantly.
John 10:10b (NKJV)

Our first home was on a corner lot, facing a major street called Headland Hills Avenue. The house was a foreclosure and had been vacant for more than a year. Just picture in your mind the yard of a home being vacant for this period of time. Oh, it was a sight to see! When we moved in, Chauncy consulted with a landscape designer, re-sodded the yard with St. Augustine grass, and watered and fertilized the grass regularly. I distinctively remember Chauncy coming home from work, changing his clothes, and going outside to work in the yard. Yes, there were times when the temperature was in the low hundreds; he was sweaty, hot, tired, frustrated, and often times didn't want to be in the yard. However, he had a vision for how he wanted the yard to look and took the necessary steps to achieve what he had envisioned. He remained consistent, committed, and focused.

It didn't happen overnight; it was through a process of time that the fruit of my husband's labor was manifested: within a few months, the yard was revitalized. It could have been featured on the front cover of *Better Homes and Gardens*. Residents as well as people driving by would frequently stop and compliment my husband on how well the yard was maintained. Others would ask, "What type of grass is it? How often do you water it? What kind of fertilizer do you use?"

In marriage, we must follow these same principles. Just as there are elements necessary for your grass to grow—fertilizer, weed killer, water, and sun—there are necessary elements for a marriage to grow: communication, commitment, time together, and the Word of God. Envision what you desire your marriage to be. Then take the necessary steps to achieve what you have envisioned. Yes, it is hard work. And yes, you may become frustrated at times. But if you remain consistent, committed, and focused, you will experience an abundant marriage by God's design.

Thought of the Week
Abundant life includes healing, nourishment, salvation, and much more. With Christ, your marriage can be that of a much higher quality of life.

Prayer of the Week
Lord, help us to realize that in order to experience abundance in marriage we must communicate, spend time together, and rely on the Word of God to mold us. Help our love to always be for You, for one another and forever. In Jesus' name, Amen.

Bridging The Gap

Reflections

Dana Fuller

~§ WEEK 2 §~

How To Cultivate Your Grass
I came that they may have and enjoy life, and have it in abundance (to the full, till it overflows).
John 10: 10b (AMP)

When choosing the type of grass one wants in their lawn, it is necessary to consider the climate in which they live. In warmer climates, one may choose Bahia, Bermuda, or St. Augustine grass. In cooler climates, one may choose Kentucky Bluegrass, Bentgrass, or Tall Fescue.

In making a grass selection that was best for our lawn when we lived in Florida, Chauncy had to consider the climate in which we lived, as well as the number of trees on our property, and how much maintenance that would be required. As a result, he chose St. Augustine grass, a grass that is deep rooted, tough, fast growing, thrives in shady areas, and is very tolerant to warm weather climate, but requires a lot of maintenance.

Now that my family and I reside in North Carolina, where the climate is much cooler, my husband's grass selection had to change. St. Augustine grass was not an option, as it cannot survive in the cooler climate. He had to choose a more suitable grass type. He chose Tall Fescue, a grass which is deep rooted, and drought tolerant but does not require as much maintenance as the St. Augustine grass.

Every marriage is different. What causes one to thrive may cause another to decline. Just as we had to change our grass selection when we moved from a warm to cool climate, we have to change in our marriages. We must change our way of thinking, our attitudes, and the way we care for one another. Most importantly, we must be willing to change with the changes. If you are not willing to adapt, then eventually your grass will die.

Thought of the Week

Ask yourself: what change do I need to make in order for my marriage to thrive?

Prayer of the Week

Dear God, give us wisdom to cultivate our marriage. Help our marriage to be deep-rooted, resilient, and vibrant, the way You designed it to be. Help us to be willing to change with the changes. Help our love to always be for You, for one another and for a lifetime. In Jesus' name, Amen.

Dana Fuller

Reflections

❧ WEEK 3 ☙

Is the Grass Really Greener on the Other Side?
*In whom all the building fitly framed together groweth
unto a holy temple in the Lord.*
Ephesians 2:21 (KJV)

Have you ever driven through certain neighborhoods and thought, "Wow! What a beautiful lawn," or "Their grass is so green, it looks artificial," or "I wish our grass looked as green as their grass looks?" My husband and I have. We would drive through neighborhoods admiring various plants, the detailed landscaping and how plush some of the yards were. On several occasions we stopped to ask what brand of fertilizer was being used and how often the grass was being watered. Our yard was green, but we desired it to be a deeper green.

So often we may compare our marriages to that of our parents, co-workers, or friends. We may look at someone else's marriage and say, "Why can't I have a marriage like they have?" My husband and I often receive compliments on our relationship. We hear comments like, "You guys act as if you're still on your honeymoon" and "You all look like you've just gotten married."

My eldest sister recently asked, "How is it that after twenty-two years of marriage, your heart still beats for your husband?"

I answered, "We never fell out of love at the same time." When I wanted to throw in the towel, he would say, "Babe, we can make it." And when he wanted to quit, I would say, "Honey, we can make it." A good marriage doesn't just happen, you must work at it. So, is the grass greener on the other side, or is it just that you are not tending to yours? Don't give up. If you tend to it, be assured it will definitely grow!

Thought of the Week

A good marriage doesn't just happen; both parties must be willing to work at it to experience a greener grass.

Prayer of the Week

Heavenly Father, refresh the soul of our marriage by sending the rain and the sunshine that will make our marriage grow and flourish. Help our love to always be for You, for one another, for a lifetime. In Jesus' name, Amen.

Bridging The Gap

Reflections

~§ WEEK 4 §~

It's Time to Take Your Yard Back!
The thief cometh not, but for to steal, and to kill, and to destroy: I am come that they might have life, and that they might have it more abundantly.
John 10:10 (KJV)

One morning on his way to work, my husband noticed small brown patches throughout the yard. Over the next few days, the small brown patches grew into large brown patches throughout our entire front yard. We later realized that our yard had been infested with an insect called the Chinch Bug. They are one of the worst lawn pests and are extremely difficult to get rid of. Chinch Bugs suck the plant juices while injecting chemicals into grass plants. If untreated, they will destroy a yard.

Chinch Bugs can destroy yards, just like the devil can destroy marriages and isn't it just like the devil to attempt to suck life out of your marriage, inject poison, conflict, and discord into your relationship? The brown patches began small, and because my husband didn't tend to them immediately, they grew, and the Chinch Bugs nearly destroyed our entire yard.

My husband became frustrated when he had to re-sod certain areas of the yard. Not only was it time consuming, but it was quite costly. But he didn't give up! He had to purchase a pesticide to treat the grass, replace the areas that were infested, and water the grass until the lawn was healthy again. Do you hear what I'm saying? Get it in your spirit! He did not talk about what needed to be done, but he took action. It's time to take action and take your marriage back! Will it be hard? Of course it will, but if you stay committed to God, then you can surely remain committed to one another.

Thought of the Week

Coming together is a beginning. Staying together is progress. Working together is success.

Prayer of the Week

Heavenly Father, help us to realize that marriage is a continuous learning process that demands work from both parties. Grant us the wisdom that we need to diffuse any discord that the enemy tries to inject into our marriage. Help our love to always be for You, for one another, and for a life time in Jesus' name, Amen.

Dana Fuller

Reflections

Weeks 5-9
TRANSFORMATION

Dana Fuller

∽ WEEK 5 ∾

Metamorphosis Encounter

Do not conform any longer to the pattern of this world, but be transformed by the renewing of your mind. Then you will be able to test and approve what God's will is— his good, pleasing and perfect will.
Romans 12:2 (NIV)

Have you ever studied the life cycle of the butterfly? What amazes me most about its life is its experience of metamorphosis. A metamorphosis is a transformation or stages in which various insects evolve. It changes from an egg, to a larva, to a pupa, and finally to an adult. This process doesn't happen overnight—in some cases, depending upon the butterfly, this TRANSFORMATION process could take up to a year!

As I reflect on my marriage over the years, I can relate to the butterfly's journey. I would pray the same prayer year after year, "God, change my husband." I was beginning to sound like a broken record, and then one day to my surprise, God responded to my prayer by asking me, "Why can't you change?"

One thing that I have learned through the years is that if you talk to God, God will talk back to you. And what a revelation it was! I was not expecting that response.

"God, what do you mean? Why can't I change? He is the one that needs to change! I don't need to change."

Were there things about my husband he needed to change? Of course, but this wasn't about me changing him, it was about me changing me. And that is exactly what I did, I changed my response to conflict, I changed my tone. I even changed my body language when we did not agree.

Like the butterfly's metamorphosis, this change in me didn't happen overnight—nothing in life is instant. Please hear me good: it was not until I acted upon what God had said that the change took place. Knowledge is power, but not until the knowledge is applied. We can always learn new ways of enhancing our marriage, but our marriage will not be enhanced until we apply what we have learned.

Thought of the Week

Change facilitates growth, and growth is necessary for change. Be willing to change with the changes to experience heaven's best in your marriage.

Prayer of the Week

Lord, help us to experience a metamorphosis in our marriage. Let us seek You for guidance of what changes each of us need to make in order to make our marriage a marriage by Your design. Help our love to always be for You, for one another and for a lifetime. In Jesus' name, Amen.

Bridging The Gap

Reflections

⊰ WEEK 6 ⊱

Empowered to Change Your Marriage
I have given you authority to trample on snakes and scorpions and to overcome all the power of the enemy; nothing will harm you.
Luke 10:19 (NIV)

Let's go back to the life cycle of the butterfly. In its earliest stages, a caterpillar matures only through consuming plant leaves, which provide essential sugar and minerals. The mother butterfly *must* lay her eggs on the type of leaf that the caterpillar will eat. Each type of caterpillar likes only certain types of leaves, and since the caterpillars are tiny and cannot travel to a new plant, they need to hatch on the kind of leaf that they need to eat.

Isn't it amazing how God designed the mother butterfly to know where to lay her eggs? She was born with this instinct to nurture and protect. Well, God has also given us the Holy Spirit which empowers us to overcome any snares that the enemy of our soul may try to create. **Change facilitates growth and growth is necessary for change. The enemy does not want you to experience growth but wants you to remain stagnant.** The snares may appear, but God will always provide a way of escape. Paul said, *I can do all things through Christ who strengtheneth me (Philippians 4:13 [KJV])*. I can change through Christ—the key words here are 'through Christ'. Yes, His unlimited power can bring wholeness and change to any marriage if both parties desire them. We have the instinct to change with the Holy Spirit's help. We must not resist the change but allow the change to take place. If we do so, our marriage will change from the caterpillar to a beautiful butterfly just the way God created it to be.

How about a little homework for this week? Your assignment is to do something for your spouse that you've never done before or something that you haven't done in a while. Here are a few suggestions:

Bridging The Gap

- Send a love letter through the mail.
- Hot shower for two.
- Breakfast in bed.
- Bubble bath for two.
- Pack your spouse a lunch.
- Hold hands.
- Give your spouse a massage.

Just have fun!

Thought of the Week
Society may renovate, but only God can recreate and bring change in your marriage.

Prayer of the Week
Dear God, we recognize that we are not perfect, but we do serve a perfect God who is able to do exceedingly abundantly above all that we ask or think, according to Your power that works in us. Thank You for inspiring us to make the necessary changes we need to make individually so that our marriage will be according to Your design. We pray that our love will always be for You, for one another, and for a lifetime. In Jesus' name, Amen.

Dana Fuller

Reflections

✥ WEEK 7 ✥

It's Time to Change
*To everything there is a season, and a time for every
matter or purpose under heaven.*
Ecclesiastes 3:1 (AMP)

My family and I were Floridians until my husband received a promotion and his job relocated us from Tampa to North Carolina in the summer of 2006. Can you imagine living in one state your entire life and everything that is familiar to you changes within a matter of months?

There were obvious changes that we recognized immediately, such as rush-hour traffic (what was considered rush-hour traffic in North Carolina would have been considered as normal in Tampa) and the fluctuations in the seasons. I vividly remember the excitement in our boys' voices one morning as they entered our bedroom and said, "Mom, have you noticed how colorful the leaves are on the trees outside?" This was something entirely different for us; we never had the opportunity to experience the different seasons in Florida.

It wasn't until we moved that we were able to experience all this. *And it will not be until you move that you will experience change in your marriage.* I can't emphasize the word 'change' enough. You must change! No, you cannot, and you will not be able to change one another, but God can change you both.

I am a living testimony that if you apply these simple principles to your marriage, it will work! Now, I'm sure some of you are saying, "Can I change or how do I change?" It's simple, pray and seek God's counsel. Yes, the principles are simple, but the process will hurt. The hurt will not come close to the fulfillment that you will experience when your marriage is one that God has designed.

There are many resources available for couples to experience abundance in their marriages. This book is one resource, but it is up to you to use the resources available: **counseling, self-help books, and the internet has a wealth of information on marriage and relationships.** If you know your marriage is in turmoil, but you fail to do anything about it, you are settling and will not experience God's best for your marriage.

Thought of the Week
Genuine change comes from within not from without.

Prayer of the Week
Dear God, help us not to resist, but to make the necessary changes that we need to make in order for our marriage to be according to Your master design. Help our love to always be for You, for one another, and for a lifetime. In Jesus' name, Amen.

Bridging The Gap

Reflections

⊰ WEEK 8 ⊱

You Can Change
I can do all things through Christ that strengtheneth me.
Philippians 4:13 (ESV)

What would you do if you had the opportunity to change the type of car you drove, the home in which you reside, or even your career choice instantly with absolutely no strings attached? Think for a moment before you answer this question. Any car, any home, or career of your choice each paid in full with no expiration date. The only thing needed is your decision. How long do you think it would take you to do that?

For some, you wouldn't have to give it a second thought. For others, it may take weeks, months, or even years. And then there are those who would say, "There is nothing wrong with the car I drive, and I've lived at this residence all of my life, why move now?" Some may say, "This has been my place of employment since high school; this is all that I know." Oh, we've heard it so often, "I've always been this way. My mom was like this, my dad was like this, this is just who I am, and I'm never going to change."

It's not that you can't change—it's that you refuse to change.

The Word of God says to grow in grace and in the knowledge of our Lord and Savior Jesus Christ **(2 Peter 3:18)**. In my book, growth implies change. Could you imagine having a baby and twenty years later you still have a baby? God designed us to grow from infancy to adulthood. He doesn't change, but He requires us to change. God understands that change is necessary for our survival. Look all around you—the world that God created changes every day, month, and year. This isn't just for the plants and animals. It's for humanity.

Bridging The Gap

Think about the seasons God created that brings about changes. If you and your spouse have been in a season of winter where your marriage has been cold the entire time; and you are no closer to becoming one unit, one team, than you were ten, fifteen, or twenty years ago then whatever you are doing isn't working. You don't need a rocket scientist to tell you that. Think about this devotion as an open book quiz for your marriage. The answers are right in front of you, now what are you going to do? My husband and I changed, will you?

Thought of the Week
Marriage is not about tolerating one another. It's about celebrating one another.

Prayer of the Week
Dear God, we denounce every negative thought that the enemies of our marriage try to plant into our relationship. We know that we both must change to experience heaven's best for our marriage. Help our love to be for You, for one another, for a lifetime. In Jesus' name, Amen.

Dana Fuller

Reflections

⊰ WEEK 9 ⊱

A Marriage Worth Fighting For
I have strength for all things in Christ who empowers me (I am ready for anything and equal to anything through Him who infuses inner strength into me; I am self-sufficient in Christ's sufficiency).
Philippians 4:13 (AMP)

Statistically speaking, every marriage has a 50/50 chance of surviving, but all marriages struggle. And our marriage was no exception to the rule. We experienced seasons of drought in our marriage that seemed to last a lifetime. The 'D' word—divorce—surfaced plenty of times in some heated arguments. The enemy of our marriage had us looking at each other and not at him.

The Word of God states, *The thief cometh not, but for to steal, and to kill, and to destroy: I am come that they might have life, and that they may have it more abundantly. (John 10:10 [KJV])* What am I saying? Our real battles are not against each other. The devil's sole purpose is to take your marriage out, but I encourage you to unite with your spouse and take the devil out. He's the real enemy, not your spouse. God has a purpose and a plan for your marriage and the enemy does not want you to fulfill it; therefore, he will use any measure necessary to cause you and your spouse to abort your destiny.

I am speaking from our experiences. We were where many of you might find yourselves right now, unhappy and ready to throw in the towel, feeling that all hope is lost, but I'm here to tell you that there is still hope and that God still performs miracles in the twenty-first century. God placed a passion in me for couples while I was in my mother's womb and the enemy tried with all his might to kill that seed. **Although I was not aware of the call, the call was on my life from conception as the Word of God states in Jeremiah 1:5a,** *Before I formed you, I knew you, before you were born,, I sanctified and ordained you. (KJV)*

Had I succumbed to the lies of the enemy, you would not be reading this devotion right now! Yes, that's all they are—lies! God has empowered us with everything we need to change, but will we change?

Thought of the Week

With God's power working in us, God can do much more than anything we can ask or imagine.

Prayer of the Week

Dear God, open our hearts to see all that You have planned for our marriage. Help us to see our marriage only through Your eyes. Help our love to always be for You, for one another, and for a lifetime. In Jesus' name, Amen.

Bridging The Gap

Reflections

Dana Fuller

Bridging The Gap

Weeks 10-15
MARRIAGE

Dana Fuller

~ WEEK 10 ~

Are You Ready to Say, "I Do?"
*A wise man will hear and increase in learning,
and a man of understanding will acquire wise counsel.*
Proverbs 1:5 (KJV)

Pre-marital counseling is extremely important before you say, "I do." My husband and I dated for about two years before he popped the famous question, "Would you marry me?" Then it was another year before we said, "I do." Pre-marital counseling wasn't offered to us. I wish it had been! I believe that had we received counseling before marriage we would have avoided plenty of the heartaches that we've since encountered. Wedding vows clearly state that marriage should not be entered into unadvisedly or lightly, but reverently, discreetly, advisedly, and solemnly. Premarital counseling does not prevent issues from occurring in your marriage, but it does equip you with the tools to handle them when they do occur.

Often we get so caught up in planning the wedding that we neglect to plan the marriage. The wedding is merely a ceremony—immediately after saying, "I do," your marriage begins, but what preparation do we make to assure the success of our marital relationship?

Many people think that premarital counseling determines whether you should or should not get married, but in actuality, counseling is designed to help you understand and talk through your differences in parenting, household chores, family budgeting, sexuality, and spirituality before entering into matrimony. Some of the questions may be personal, but it's vital to address these issues before entering into holy matrimony.

Marriage is ordained by God and those partaking in marriage should be willing to honor marriage as God honors marriage. You should be willing to take the vows seriously and abide by the guidelines that God has set for marriage. If God's guidelines are followed, couples can experience love and marriage by His design.

Thought of the Week
Plans fail for lack of counsel, but with many advisers they succeed.

Prayer of the Week
Dear God, help us seek Your divine counsel before entering holy matrimony. Help our marriage to be healthy, built on honesty, trust, and commitment. Help our love to always be for You, for one another, and for a lifetime. In Jesus' name, Amen.

Bridging The Gap

Reflections

✦ WEEK 11 ✦

Questions to Ask Before (and After) Marriage
*Listen to advice and accept instruction
that you may gain wisdom in your future.*
Proverbs 19:20 (ESV)

My husband and I have hosted an annual couple's Christmas dinner for the past few years. The night is filled with fun, games, gifts, and laughter. One particular year, we played the Newlywed Game. In this game, the men were taken into another room and asked various questions about their wives, such as: What is her favorite color? What is her dream car? What makes her angry? These were things they were supposed to know about their spouses. To our surprise, most of the couples knew very little about one another's likes, dislikes, dreams, and admirations.

To work toward the success of your marriage, and help you understand your differences before saying "I do," there are several questions couples may ask each other before marrying, including:

1. Do you want children? If so, how many?
2. Will we keep separate accounts?
3. Are you a tither?
4. How often will we have sex a week?
5. How will we discipline the children?

I've listed only a few, but the list goes on and on. The key is to not evade questions and concerns that pertain to your marriage. Often couples say, "Oh, we'll deal with it when it comes." Well, that is true. But if you discuss the questions before marrying, when you are faced with situations, you are more apt to handle them in the appropriate manner without having unnecessary drama. So discuss the questions before marrying when you are able to and not after marrying when you may have to.

And for those reading who are already married, now is the time to check back in with these questions! How well would you do on the Newlywed Game?

Thought of the Week
Ask the right questions if you are going to find the right answers. Vanessa Redgrave

Prayer of the Week
Dear God, help us seek Your divine counsel before entering holy matrimony. Help our marriage to be healthy, built on honesty, trust, and commitment. Help our love to always be for You, for one another, and for a lifetime. In Jesus' name, Amen.

Dana Fuller

Reflections

❧ WEEK 12 ☙

Covenant Versus a Contract

The LORD hath been witness between you and the wife of your youth, against whom you have dealt treacherously: yet is she your companion, and the wife of your covenant.
Malachi 2:14 (KJV)

When my husband and I celebrated twenty-three year of marriage, I reflected on our covenant vows. Many may ask, how did we survive marriage for this length of time? Well, I'll be the first to tell you that it wasn't easy. There were plenty of times when we didn't feel like we were in love with one another, but we learned through staying committed to our covenant vows to God that love isn't about what you feel, but what you *do*. Love truly does cover a multitude of faults.

Many couples view marriage as a contract rather than a covenant; and there is a big difference. A *contract* is what you sign for your cell phone, a personal loan, or an apartment. A *covenant* is a promise made in the presence of God. Remember the one who presided over your wedding? If you were married in a church by a pastor, they were there as a representative of God. And your vows: there are many versions but all virtually the same meaning:

> *"Dearly beloved we are gathered here today in the sight of God and man." During the exchanging of the vows you were asked the following: "[Name], do you take [Name] to be your wedded [husband/wife] to live together in marriage. Do you promise to love, comfort, honor and keep him/her for better or worse, for richer or poorer, in sickness and in health. And forsaking all others, be faithful to him/her only so long as you both shall live?"*

Throughout marriage, you will have different seasons—seasons where you may not have a lot of money, for instance. But the vows do not state for richer or for richer, they state for richer or for poorer. You may not have a lot of money for many years, but you must still remain faithful and committed to your spouse until God blesses you to have an abundance in your finances.

The minister also asked if you would remain faithful in sickness and in health. During the wedding ceremony, many say, "I do," but don't fully realize that their spouse may become sick. Many only see the now—the healthy spouse they can't imagine ever becoming sick. Many are caught off guard when their spouse becomes ill and remains ill for a length of time. What does one do during the time when their spouse is ill? You remember your vows: you remain committed in sickness and in health.

Throughout the different seasons that you encounter in your marriage, don't forget the vows that you made to your spouse and to God: to remain faithful in all seasons.

Thought of the Week
Covenant vows are never vows of contentment but commitment.

Prayer of the week
Dear God, help us to realize marriage is a sacred covenant made between You and our spouse. Help us to reflect on our vows and remain faithful to them. Help our love to always be for You, for one another and for a lifetime. In Jesus' name, Amen.

Bridging The Gap

Reflections

Dana Fuller

⊰ WEEK 13 ⊱

We're Married, Now What? Making Time for Each Other
So guard yourself in your spirit and do not break faith with your wife (husband) of your Youth. I hate divorce says the Lord God of Israel.
Malachi 2:15b -16a (NIV)

My husband and I met at a Gospel concert in Jacksonville, Florida. Was it love at first sight? No, and to be quite honest, it wasn't even 'like' at first sight. **My husband was not my type. I had always been attracted to tall men and my husband was short—there was no attraction whatsoever, not to mention the fact that I found him to be a male chauvinist.** He told me later that because of the way I dressed, he thought I was old fashioned, plain, and would become an old lady in a rocking chair never to marry.

I'm sure many of you have heard the phrase "opposites attract." Well, that was the way we were, different as night and day, oil, and vinegar. Chauncy believed in saving, saving, saving, and I, on the other hand, believed in spending, spending, spending!

So, no I didn't see stars, and no, the Earth didn't shake. Our relationship started out as friends. I lived in Clearwater, Florida and he resided in Gainesville, Florida. Soon after the concert in Jacksonville, Chauncy relocated to Tampa, about forty-five minutes from where I lived. We would see each other at events at one of our sister churches of our organization and we began talking and our relationship grew from there. Our friendship led to dating, and two years after that we were married.

But as I stated earlier, it wasn't love at first sight. There are three loves defined from the Greek language. These loves are Eros love (sexual love or desire), Philia love (a friendship love arriving from close association), and Agape love (the love God has for man and the love mankind has for God and other humans). Though all three are needed for any marital relationship, our final destination is to reach the Agape love, for it is this love that will enable us to experience happily-ever-after.

When Chauncy and I were dating, we didn't get to see each other often because at the time he worked full-time and was a full-time student. This inconvenience did not stop us; GTE (the local telephone company at that time) was at our disposal, and we took full advantage of it. We would talk until two or three in the morning; both sleepy and tired, we just enjoyed hearing the other's voice. One night, I actually fell asleep while he was talking and was awakened to the sound of a dial tone! Just hearing the sound of his voice made me feel that he was near.

Take a moment to reflect on how you felt toward your husband/wife when you were dating, how you loathed to be without them and desired to be in their presence every waking moment. Think about the excitement you felt when you would hear their voice, the chills that ran through your body from their touch. Just reflect! Think back to all the dining out, drive-in movies, picnics at the park, the love letters that some of you still may have tucked away. Reflect on what attracted you to the one who you were facing when you uttered the words, "I do."

So how can I keep the romance kindled in my marriage, you ask? What can you do to keep the fire burning in your relationship? There is no mysterious love potion or chant. It's simple: follow what you did when you first met. Held hands, night walks in the park, dining at your favorite restaurant, banana splits at Baskin & Robbins, etc. Need I say more? No matter how busy your week may be, always remember to make time for each other. My husband and I are both busy, but now that our boys are older, we generally go to Garage Sales and then to breakfast every Saturday morning. We both enjoy and look forward to spending this time together since it is "our" time.

Thought of the Week

Your marriage is like a garden, what you plant will determine your Harvest.

Prayer of the Week

Dear God, we reaffirm our commitment to each other and the vows we made to You. We promise to love and cherish each other all the days of our lives for better or for worse. Help our love to always be for You, for one another and for a lifetime, in Jesus' name, Amen.

Bridging The Gap

Reflections

Dana Fuller

∽ WEEK 14 ∾

What Makes a Solid Foundation?
So everyone who hears these words of mine and act upon them (obeying them) will be like a sensible (prudent, practical, wise) man who built his house upon a rock.
Matthew 7:24 (AMP)

Having a home built is something that everyone should have the opportunity to experience. I remember this event as if it were yesterday: Our realtor had taken us to view several homes, but nothing really stood out with us. We were at the point of giving up until she said there was a new subdivision she wanted us to see. The location was a disadvantage—it was in an entirely different city, about forty-five minutes from my place of employment and fifty minutes from my husband's job—but as soon as we walked into the model home named 'Destiny' (after looking through several others), we knew this was the home for us.

Imagine the excitement we both felt going out to the property for the ground breaking and laying of the foundation. My husband took pictures of every step of this process, and I do mean every step—everything from the ground breaking, to the laying of the foundation, to the hanging of the dry wall!

A good foundation provides stability for the entire structure and is essential for the longevity of any building. Just as every building needs a strong foundation if it's going to stand, so does every marriage. There are basically three types of foundations: slab, crawlspace, and basement. A slab foundation is one in which there is absolutely no space near the house foundation. It's an ideal foundation in regions where the water can get really high above the ground. A crawl space foundation is available in places where the soil texture is incredibly soft and cannot hold much weight. There is a small space between the ground and the first level of the house. A basement foundation offers excellent protection from severe weather. A basement foundation can add valuable additional living space to a home. Homes built on basement foundations are stronger than others, especially ones simply built on a slab. They also have a better resale value.

No foundation is any better than the other, but it takes the same principles to arrive at a complete product. Each foundation is available to a buyer, but there are reasons why a foundation would be more suitable than another: climate, soil, and the buyer's preference. Just as in a marriage there may be other foundations one may build upon, **like education, family, money, and status,** but the best marriage to endure the storms of life is the marriage that is centered on Christ. Storms may wail against all three of the foundations, but if the contractor has done their homework, the storms may break the windows or blow off doors, but the foundation will remain intact. Yes, there may be disagreements and misunderstandings in a marriage, but if it is Christ-centered; one based on prayer, love, and respect, it <u>WILL</u> withstand any storm.

Thought of the Week
A marriage, like a home, is only as strong as its foundation.

Prayer of the Week
Dear God, help us to rely on You as our skillful master builder in our marriages. Thank You for establishing a firm foundation for marriage from the beginning of time. Help our love to always be for You, for one another, and for a lifetime. In Jesus' name, Amen.

Dana Fuller

Reflections

⊰ WEEK 15 ⊱

Thank You God for Our Marriage
*In everything give thanks: for this is the will
of God in Christ Jesus concerning you.
1 Thessalonians 5:18*

"Thank you" is often heard when a waiter/waitress gives a customer a menu, when a door is opened for someone, or when someone receives a gift. We use the words 'Thank You' at least once during the course of a day, and this is great—we should always exemplify an attitude of appreciation without hesitation. It's easy to focus on the negative things about our spouse, but it is just as easy to reflect and thank God for their strengths.

Here is a prayer that you may want to add to your library of prayers:

> *Dear God, we declare that You are Lord in our marriage, and we thank You that our marriage is yoked together with You. Thank You for teaching us everything that we need to know about our spouse and for infusing us to minister to one another's physical, emotional, and spiritual needs. Thank You that our relationship is Christ-centered and not self-centered, we appreciate You being with us in the ups and downs of our marriage, for better or worse, for richer or for poorer, in sickness and in health. Thank You for teaching us that every great relationship begins with You.*

Thought of the Week
Being grateful for the small, positions you for the greater.

Prayer of the Week
Dear God, thank You for deepening our relationship within our marriage. We pray not our will, but Your will be done in us and through us. Help our love to always be for You, for one another, and for a lifetime. In Jesus' name, Amen.

Dana Fuller

Reflections

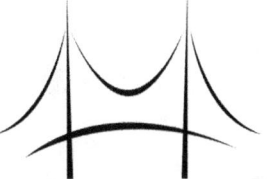

Weeks 16-20
IT'S WORTH THE WORK

Dana Fuller

Bridging The Gap

✥ WEEK 16 ✥

Is It Time to Shift Gears?
So guard yourself in your spirit and do not break faith with your wife (husband) of your Youth. I hate divorce says the Lord God of Israel.
Malachi 2:15b -16a (NIV)

My husband, Chauncy, has always been biased concerning cars with manual transmissions. He says, "Cars that have manual transmissions are more fun to drive and cars that have automatic transmissions are a little boring." I personally think that cars that have manual transmissions are a bit much, and who wants to do all of that shifting anyway!

Upon meeting and marrying my husband, I had never driven a car that did not have an automatic transmission. My first lesson driving a car that had a manual transmission was in the parking lot of St. Petersburg Junior College in Clearwater, Florida. I'm not sure who was more frightened, my husband or me. I thought that I would never master shifting gears and engaging the gas pedal at the same time. I'm surprised we both didn't get whiplash due to all of the stopping and jerking. After church service one Sunday, after practicing for months, my husband said it was time for me to go on the open highway. I didn't think that I was ready but took the wheel of the pickup truck anyway and to my surprise, I was actually doing fine! That is, until I had to stop at a red light that was on the top of a hill. One of the Deacons from the church was right on my tail. His presence threw me for a loop. My heart beat rapidly and at that very moment, I forgot everything Chauncy taught me concerning stopping on a hill. I began to roll back, and then I remembered how I had to ease off the clutch and press the gas pedal at the same time.

Just as in a marriage, I hear the spirit of the Lord saying, "It's time for a shift in your marriage!" Ask yourself, what gear is your marriage in?

If it is in neutral, it doesn't have to stay there. I remember a time when our marriage was in neutral and I'm not talking about a few weeks, or even months. I'm talking years. Chauncy dreaded coming home just as much as I dreaded him coming home. There were days when we didn't talk to one another, and when we did, we said only a few words. We even went through a season in our marriage where we didn't like each other. We weren't connecting, but praise be to God who always causes us to win, even when we don't feel like we are winning. If we are in Christ Jesus, we win! You have the keys to your car just as you do to your marriage, but it's up to you to use them. You can stay in neutral if you want, but you will never move forward in your marriage. You have the right to shift gears, and you have the right to drive forward. Will you?

Marriages may be different, but they must have the same core values to operate. Husbands and wives must love and value themselves, one another, and God. Both automatic and manual transmissions must shift to move, the question remains, "What gear will you shift to?"

Thought of the Week
It's not about where you have been in your marriage, but it's about where you are going!

Prayer of the Week
Dear God, We pray that You draw us closer to You and to one another, rekindle the fire and passion between us, help us to be willing to shift when You say shift. Help our love to always be for You, for one another and for a lifetime, in Jesus' name, Amen.

Bridging The Gap

Reflections

~ WEEK 17 ~

Shifting Out of Park
I can do all things through Christ who strengtheneth me.
Philippians 4:13 (KJV)

Imagine for a moment: you purchase a car, you are given the keys, you drive the car home, park it, and never drive it again. How ridiculous does that sound? Well, it's the same concerning your marriage. It's easy to plan your wedding, to say, "I do," to go on your honeymoon, return home, and then do absolutely nothing upon your return! It's easy for a loving, committed relationship to stall out and you refuse to shift the car from park to drive. Let's be real, I'm not saying your marriage will operate in drive 24/7, but I am saying don't expect to experience abundance in your marriage if you cannot utilize all the gears in your car. Park, reverse, neutral, and drive—one gear is no more important than the other; each has its own significance. I think of these gears as seasons, and my husband and I have experienced all of them.

It seemed as though we remained in park for years. Our views on child rearing were different as well as our views on marriage, finances, and life. However, we had a common denominator and that was Christ. Remember you are not the first couple to experience ups and downs in your relationship, and you will not be the last. But Paul wrote in Philippians 4:13, *"I can do all things through Christ which strengtheneth me."* (KJV) This scripture states, "All" things, not just some things, so both husbands and wives can be what God wants them to be.

True sufficiency is found in the strength of Christ, so when the enemy of my marriage comes in like a flood, Christ's strength is all sufficient.

Thought of the Week
In order to move, we must shift.

Bridging The Gap

Prayer of the Week

Dear God, infuse our love for You and one another. We know that You are the all-sufficient one in our marriage. Help us to embrace the significance of every season. Help our love to always be for You, one another, and for a lifetime. In Jesus' name, Amen.

Dana Fuller

Reflections

⋘ WEEK 18 ⋙

Gears are Like the Seasons
And we know that all things work together for good to them that love God, to them who are the called according to his purpose.
Romans 8:28 (KJV)

When I think of gears in a car, whether it's an automatic or manual transmission, I immediately think of the four seasons: summer, fall, winter and spring. Now, I'm sure some of you are saying, "Why does she think about seasons when she thinks about gears?" Well, let's see.

Seasons bring about change, and so do gears in a car. Four seasons, four gears. Each gear and season have a specific purpose. As I stated in last week's devotion, my husband and I have experienced all four seasons in our marriage. There was purpose in every season, but we couldn't see it because we were so stuck on *I: I deserve better. I can't do this anymore. I want out. I* knew the word and so did my husband.

Oh, we had many people prophesy into our lives: "God has a great work for you all in marriage ministry." "Your stumbling blocks are mere stepping stones to where God is taking you all," and "Your experiences will have a great impact on other marriages." Yet the enemy of our marriage had the upper hand because we were stuck in one season.

How ridiculous would one look wearing a fur coat, scarf, and hat in the summer? How about wearing shorts and a T-shirt in the winter when the temperature is ten degrees below freezing? Each season is a process and one should seek God for direction. That's what my husband and I finally did; we sought God for direction and then applied scripture to our season. We were stuck in one gear and it seemed as though we could not move, until God spoke to my husband

and said that if he didn't change his attitude towards me, we would not experience abundance in our marriage.

Now, don't misunderstand me, in that drought season we still took care of our responsibilities. We both took care of each other and the children. I did not stop cooking and cleaning because we were stuck in a gear, and my husband didn't stop mowing the grass and washing our cars. We still worked as a team during those years. When a car becomes stuck in a gear for a long time, it can cause major damage to the transmission. If you are stuck in one particular season for a long time, it may cause major damage to your marriage. Don't get stuck in the "I" season because there is no "I" in "TEAM." Be the team that God has designed you to be!

Thought of the Week
The greatest knowledge is to know the will of the Lord, but the greatest endeavor is to do it.

Prayer of the Week
Dear God, help us not only to know Your Word but to apply Your Word to our marriage. As we experience the different seasons in our marriage, help our love to always be for You, one another and for a lifetime in Jesus' name, Amen.

Bridging The Gap

Reflections

✥ WEEK 19 ✥

If It's Broken, Fix It

Now to Him who is able to do exceedingly abundantly above all we ask or think, according to the power that works in us.
Ephesians 3:20 (NKJV)

A friend of my husband and his family, whom we hadn't seen in more than thirteen years, relocated to South Carolina about several years ago. When my husband and his friend corresponded with one another, they would often talk about us getting together, but our schedules just wouldn't allow it. Out of nowhere, my husband received a call that they wanted to come visit us during the Labor Day weekend. Once they arrived, we had a lot of catching up to do. We reminisced about old times and shared how we each met our spouses. I asked my husband if he had told his friend that we had an online marriage ministry. He hadn't. Our friend and his wife visited the website and proceeded to read the devotion for the week. His wife and I had several good conversations about marriage; I shared some of our struggles and how we triumphed over them, how it took the both of us changing in order to experience heaven's best in our marriage, and how I remembered saying, "We'll never become one at the rate we were going!"

She turned to me and asked, "How long did it take for you two to become one?" I paused for a moment and said, "Chauncy and I have been married for twenty-two years, and I can truly say that we have only walked in oneness the last five years of our marriage."

That's right, only five years, and they have been the best! I'm sure some of you are saying, "How can she write the things that she writes or share such personal information about her marriage?" Well, my response to that is, "How can I not share if it may help someone?"

Bridging The Gap

Couples are dealing with real life issues in their marriages, but the church does not want to address them, and as a result, the divorce rate in the church is at an overwhelming high. If something is broken in your home, wouldn't you have it repaired? Well, that's exactly what we did. Our marriage was broken, and God gave us insight through His Word. Through us seeking His guidance on how to fix it, we were able to repair our marriage. Rest assured, we didn't become fixed overnight, it was a process and because we were both willing to submit to the process, we are a living testimony that the Word of God does work if you apply it.

Everything that we need is in the Word of God. We both brought baggage into our marriage, and we both needed to be fixed. My husband was a hard worker and a wonderful provider, yet totally disconnected from me when it came to meeting my emotional needs. I, on the other hand, lived at home with my parents until approximately a year before I was married at the age of twenty-six. I would give my parents $100 a month and the rest of my pay check was for me to spend on whatever I wanted. If I wanted something, I purchased it. If you were to mention the word 'savings' to me, my response would be, "What's that?"

Yes, we were broken, but when we realized the power that we both possessed through working the Word in our marriage, restoration was set into motion. Paul tells us in Ephesians 3:20, *"Now to Him who is able to do exceedingly abundantly above all that we ask or think according to the power that works in us."* (NKJV) This is confirmation that we are equipped and empowered through the Word of God to overcome any and all obstacles that the enemy of our marriage may present.

Thought of the Week
It doesn't matter what length of time your marriage has been broken. Whatever is broken in your marriage CAN be fixed.

Dana Fuller

Prayer of the Week

Dear God, we realize through Your Word we are empowered to fix whatever is broken in our marriage. Help us to move from a self-centered marriage into a Christ-centered marriage. Help our love to be for You, for one another and for a lifetime. In Jesus' name, Amen.

Bridging The Gap

Reflections

Dana Fuller

∞§ WEEK 20 §∞

Don't Settle

In all thy ways acknowledge Him and He shall direct thy paths.
Proverbs 3:6 (KJV)

How many of you remember your very first car? I remember mine as if it were yesterday: it was a 1980 yellow four-door Toyota Corona; I don't think they make them anymore. I was extremely proud of it. It was old yet exceptionally reliable. It actually reminded me of the cars that the clowns would ride in at the circus. Remember? And all the clowns would step out of the car? Well, that's what my car looked like, but it was mine and it was paid for. I drove this car for several years until one day it just stopped running. I could have had it serviced over and over again, but I knew it was time to purchase another vehicle.

Now, think about your first apartment. My husband and I's first apartment was a one-bedroom, one-bathroom apartment. In order to get to the bathroom, you had to go through the bedroom—very awkward. Yes, it was small in size, but it was quaint, had character and we made it our home. It was never in our minds to just settle into this apartment for the rest of our lives. We resided there for two years and then moved into a two-bedroom, two-bathroom apartment and then into our first house, which had three bedrooms, two bathrooms, a split bedroom plan with a fireplace, formal living and dining rooms, a screen patio and an over-sized two-car garage on a corner lot. We chose not to settle into that one-bedroom studio apartment, just as we chose not to settle for just being married to avoid the divorce.

People are ambitious concerning the things that they desire in life (such as purchasing their dream car or home; or becoming the vice president of a corporation) and they stop at nothing until they succeed. To pay off an average car it takes about five to six years, depending upon your financing. To pay off an average house mortgage you can choose a 15-

or a 30-year mortgage. The average career requires at least four years of college, and if it's in the medical field, it's even longer. No matter how frustrated one may become, giving up is not an option. If you want it bad enough, you will do whatever is necessary to reach your goal. Wow, this is what I call commitment! Why can't we exhibit the same or even a greater level of patience and commitment when it comes to our marriages? Don't settle for talking about what's wrong with your marriage because change will never come, trust me!

Everything we purchase in the 21st century comes with a manual, from a vacuum cleaner to a car, and if it doesn't come with one, Google it and there you will find the operation instructions. Well, I have news for you: there is also a manual that will instruct, guide, and teach you how to experience happily-ever-after in your marriage, and that manual is the Holy Bible. Contained in the Holy Bible is everything that you need that pertains to life and godliness.

Don't just settle for being married but reach for happily-ever-after. Don't settle for being a good wife but become a virtuous one. Don't settle for being a good mother but strive to be a godly mother. Don't settle for being a good husband, but press to be the Priest, Protector, and Provider. Let me say it again, DON'T SETTLE! You didn't settle after that first car or apartment, so don't settle for defeat in your marriage. Speak life into your marriage and surround yourself with people who are like-minded.

Thought of the Week
Your marriage is like a tea bag, you never know how strong it is until it is put into hot water. What you want exists. Don't settle until you get it.

Prayer of the Week
Heavenly Father, we knowledge You as Lord in our marriage, and we thrust ourselves into the plan that You have for us. Help us to realize that there are no problems in our marriage that we may encounter that

are bigger than You. Help our love to always be for You, for one another, and for a life time. In Jesus' name, Amen.

Bridging The Gap

Reflections

Dana Fuller

Bridging The Gap

Weeks 21-26
LISTEN: TO GOD, TO YOUR MARRIAGE, AND TO EACH OTHER

Dana Fuller

∽ WEEK 21 ∾

Frequency

*Relish life with the spouse you love,
each and every day of your precarious life. Each day is God's gift.
It's all you get in exchange for your hard work of staying alive.*
Ecclesiastes 9:9 (MSG)

My favorite radio station to listen to is K-Love, a Christian radio network that features artists like Matthew West, Jeremy Camp, and Chris Tomlin. They also share positive and encouraging stories each day and offer an abundance of resources to help you grow as a Christian. There is plenty of bad news in the world, so it's refreshing to turn the radio to K-LOVE each morning for some encouraging news. I listen every morning on my way to work and I can't begin to tell you how a simple inspiring word, a song, or a listener's story has helped me to stay focused throughout my day.

One particular morning, I turned my radio on as usual to K-Love, but all I could hear was static. I pushed the station seek button several times trying to find K-Love, thinking that maybe I was on the wrong frequency, but to no avail. When I arrived at work, I shared what had happened with a coworker, and she said that K-Love can be picked up on another frequency. I was ecstatic. It also made me think about the science fiction movie called "Frequency." In it, a rare atmospheric phenomenon occurs that allows a New York City firefighter to connect with his son 30 years in the future via a short-wave radio. The son uses this opportunity to warn his father of his impending death in a warehouse fire and manages to save his father's life. In doing so, he changes history, which includes the murder of his mother. In the film, the father and son must work together, 30 years apart, to find the murderer before he strikes so they can change history again.

Are you and your spouse on the same frequency or is there static? The enemy of your marriage's sole purpose is to cause the frequency of your marriage to be distorted. Just as it took the father and son in the movie working together as a team, it will take you and your spouse coming together in order to be tuned in to the same frequency. In the movie, they thought several times that they wouldn't be able to reach one another on the frequency, but they never gave up. Often there were times when they were unable to tune into the same frequency, and the father would say, "Son, are you there?" There would be a moment of silence because of the static from the radio frequency, and then suddenly the son would say, "Yes, I'm here." There may be moments in your marriage where there is static—continue to adjust until you are on the same frequency. The father and son never gave up because they were working together for a common goal, they had to change history. You and your spouse must work together to secure your present and your future. Destiny waits for your marriage to be all that God has designed it to be.

Thought of the Week
Becoming in sync with the right frequency ensures the success of a marriage according to the Master's design.

Prayer of the Week
Dear God, help us to be tuned in to one another. Realign us to the frequency that You have designed for our marriage. Help our love to always be for You, for one another, and for a lifetime. In Jesus' name, Amen.

Bridging The Gap

Reflections

Dana Fuller

∽ WEEK 22 ∾

God Can Put It Back Together
He healeth the broken in heart, and bindeth up their wounds.
Psalms 147:3 (KJV)

There are at least one-hundred-and-twelve traditional nursery rhymes on record. One of my favorites is Humpty Dumpty. I'm sure you remember it. It went something like this: "Humpty Dumpty sat on the wall, Humpty Dumpty had a great fall! All the king's horses, and all the king's men, couldn't put Humpty together again!" I like this particular nursery rhyme because it reminds me of my husband and I's marriage. It had fallen into a state of disarray. I guess you could say as far as the East is from the West, that's how divided we had become in our relationship. Our marriage was broken into tiny pieces just as Humpty Dumpty. The enemy of our marriage had put barriers between us that appeared to be unbreakable. Although we both had issues in the marriage, I felt my husband's issues were greater than mine. So, I attempted to fix him. I became an uncertified mechanic for my husband issues, but to no travail. In the process, we became mere roommates going through the motions of life. Don't get me wrong, we remained friends during our seasons of disarray, but this wasn't marriage according to God's master plan.

Nursery rhymes are like superheroes—there is a lot that is not real about them. The king's horses and men couldn't put Humpty together again, just as I could not fix my husband, and my husband and I could not fix our marriage alone. But the King of Kings can put your marriage back together again, and that is exactly what He did for our marriage. Have you ever heard the saying, "If it's not broken, don't fix it?" Well that wasn't the case with us. Our marriage was broken to what appeared to be beyond repair. It wasn't until we stopped trying to fix one other and yielded our wills to the King's will, that our marriage began to shape into a marriage according to God's master design.

Thought of the Week
The end of our self is our beginning place in God.

Prayer of the Week
Dear God, we acknowledge You as King of Kings in our marriage. Fix what is broken in our relationship. Mend every thought, action, and will. Help our love to always be for You, for one another, and for a lifetime. In Jesus' name, Amen.

Dana Fuller

Reflections

Bridging The Gap

✥ WEEK 23 ✥

Bigger, Better, and Stronger
I shall not die, but live, and declare the works of the Lord.
Psalms 118: 17 (KJV)

Remember the 1970s television series "The Six Million Dollar Man," a sci-fi action adventure starring Lee Majors? He portrayed Steve Austin, an astronaut who was seriously injured in a test flight, and as a result was given artificial (or bionic) replacements for his legs, his right arm and one eye, leaving him with superhuman speed, strength, and telescopic vision.

Lindsay Wagner played Jaime Summers, a former tennis pro, who was introduced as Steve's childhood sweetheart in a two-part episode titled, "The Bionic Woman." In that episode, the two went sky diving, during which Jaime's parachute ripped in mid-air, and caused her to plunge to the ground. Her injuries were critical: she suffered major damage to both of her legs, one of her arms and her right ear. She was given bionic limbs similar to Steve's; unfortunately, Jaime's body rejected her new bionic limbs and her character later died after starring in only two episodes. The fans' response to her character dying off the show was so overwhelming that the producers brought her back to life in an episode titled, "The Return of the Bionic Woman." It had been discovered, it seems, that Jaime hadn't really died, but had been put into cryogenic suspension (frozen) until she could be cured.

Although this TV series was fictional, there are lessons we can apply to our marriages, such as overcoming any and every obstacle we may encounter from the enemy of our marriage. Jaime's character was brought back to life through the power of storytelling. In the same way, God can bring what appears to be dead back to life in your marriage. There were times in our marriage that my husband and I both felt as if every part of our marriage was broken and crushed without a cure in sight. When we allow the Word of God to undergo surgery on our marriages, we still must do our part to ensure that the rehabilitation process is set into motion. What am I saying? Well, Jaime and Steve went through extensive rehabilitation. They had strenuous exercises that they had to follow daily to strengthen their new bionic limbs, and we have the Word of God that we must exercise daily in our life to be equipped for any snares that the enemy of our marriage may present.

Have you ever heard the term "to flatline?" It's when no electrical activity, motion or movement is going on in the heart that a heart monitor can pick up, My husband and I experienced a flatline in our marriage several times, and we finally said, enough is enough. We wanted to experience marriage according to God's design, so we allowed God to administer CPR on us. He did the chest compressions, but it wasn't until He breathed the breath of life into us that our hearts began to beat once again for one another. Just as God breathed into Adam's nostrils the breath of life and Adam became a living soul **(Genesis 2:7)**, He can breathe life into your marriage. Your marriage shall not die but it shall live. Just as Steve and Jaime's body parts had to be rebuilt, our marriages can be rebuilt to become bigger, better, and stronger.

Thought of the Week
What greater thing is there but for two human souls to feel joined together for life?

Prayer of the Week
Dear God, we rely on You to rebuild, reconstruct all that is broken in our marriage. Help our love to always be for You, for one another, and for a lifetime. In Jesus' name, Amen.

Bridging The Gap

Reflections

✧ WEEK 24 ✧

Falling in Love?

Many waters cannot quench love; neither can floods drown it: If a man would give all the substance of his house for love, it would utter be condemned.
Song of Solomon 8:7 (KJV)

I've heard this saying for as long as I can remember, "I'm falling in love," and if you are reading this devotion, I'm sure you have heard it as well. Yes, you can meet someone, and they just take your breath away. Your heart rate increases not just from their touch, but it could be a glance, or a wink of an eye, just thinking about them sends lightning bolts throughout your entire body. My husband has a lazy eye. When he becomes tired, it's even more noticeable, at least it is to me. But when we were dating, he would glance at me, then wink—it was such a turn on for me. My entire body would melt. Okay, enough of that! There is an instant strong connection, you complete one another's, sentences, you just cannot stop thinking about that person, you feel like you're falling hopelessly in love. As some might say, "you've had a head on collision with love."

But is that love? Do we really fall in love? We fall in lust, we can fall in infatuation, and you can fall into amazing chemistry, but do you we fall in love? If we can fall in love, chances are we would fall out of love. I believe love is discovered and that takes time. You discover things that you like and dislike, you discover their strengths and their weaknesses.

You peel layers to discover their moods, how they deal with challenging situations, discover their turn on language, as well as their turn off language, and trust me, we all have them. And the good thing about discovering one another, is that it is on-going, there is no expiration date on it. We are always growing and changing. Change facilitates growth and growth is necessary for change. Thirty plus years later, Chauncy and I are yet discovering love together, and it is beautiful.

Thought of the Week
Love is discovered, and when you think you have discovered it all, you keep discovering, discovering, discovering.

Prayer of the Week
God of love, thank You for the love You have implanted in us for You and each other. Infuse the passion and wisdom to forever move forward, as we grow and discover love in our covenant union. May our love always be for You, for one another, and for a lifetime. In Jesus' name, Amen.

Dana Fuller

Reflections

WEEK 25

Follow the Directions

Receive instructions in wise dealings and the discipline of wise thoughtfulness, righteousness justice and integrity, that prudence may be given to the simple, and knowledge, discretion, and discernment to the youth.
Proverbs 1:3,4 (AMP)

I do believe I am one of the world's worst individuals when it comes to following directions. Recently, I went to Walmart to purchase racks to hang articles of clothing for a garage sale that we were having. I proceeded to assemble the racks thinking, "How difficult can it be to assemble two racks with only ten to twelve pieces per rack?" Well, needless to say, when I was finished, the racks didn't resemble the picture on the box. My husband, in passing, stopped, and glanced at them for a moment. I said, "I don't know what happened." Of course his response was, "Did you follow the directions?" I muttered a faint, "No, I didn't."

Chauncy goes right to the directions regardless of what it is; from administering medication to putting new foot paddles on our son's bicycles and assembling furniture. One year for Father's Day, I purchased him some office furniture from Office Depot. He had been admiring a particular set for a while, so I purchased and had it delivered to our home the week before Father's Day. The only catch was that the entire set would be delivered unassembled. Wow! The set consisted of a computer desk with a hutch and drawers on each side, and several book shelves. The very first thing my husband did was read the directions. It took him several weeks to complete this project, but it was well worth it. You can't go wrong if you follow the directions.

The Word of God gives specific instructions to husbands and wives. It instructs husbands to love their wives even as Christ loved the church and gave himself for it. The Bible also instructs men to love their wives as their own bodies. A husband's love should be sacrificial, nourishing, cherishing, and protective. Can you see the pattern contained in the scripture in admonishing husbands to love? Sometimes this doesn't come easy for men. "Why?" you may ask. So often when men are boys, they are told, "Don't cry" when they fall, or "Get up, you are not a baby." We don't realize we have caused our boys to suppress their feelings; therefore, when they become men it's hard for them to express emotions.

The Bible instructs wives to submit themselves to their own husbands as unto the Lord. That's right ladies, **I did say submit and there is no need to grit your teeth.** So many marriages have dissolved because we have incorrect instructions regarding this word. I've heard it oh so often, "I'll never let a man tell me what to do." We have to examine who defined the word 'submission' for each of us. Was it from Mom, Dad, or a friend? I'm here to tell you if it didn't derive from the Word of God, then it is a lie! Some believe that submission means to simply obey and to deny one's desires, and dreams, and if a wife shares her opinion with her husband then she is not submissive. This is a false concept of submission. A wife's submission to her husband is in response to her love and devotion to the Lord first. She submits to the Lord out of a humble heart, not out of fear, but her submission is voluntary.

Following directions is imperative when administering medications and assembling furniture. There are benefits from following the directions: the proper dosage is given for medication and the furniture is assembled correctly. In our marriages, if we follow the directions according to God's Word, then we experience a marriage according to God's design.

Thought of the Week
You can avoid many obstacles by just following the directions.

Bridging The Gap

Prayer of the Week

Dear God, help us to respond to every direction that You give us concerning our marriage. Help our love to always be for You, one another, and for a lifetime. In Jesus' name, Amen.

Dana Fuller

Reflections

∽ WEEK 26 ∾

What Are You Hearing?
I can do all things through Christ which strengtheneth me.
Philippians 4:13 (KJV)

Have you ever suffered from an ear infection? Ear infections are all so common among children. The latest research indicates that when a young child has a cold, an ear infection usually follows sixty-one percent of the time. For adults, there are several reasons why an ear infection may surface. A cold and post nasal drip can cause fluid buildup in the inner ear. If the infection is detected early, the infection may be more easily dealt with. If ignored, complications may occur such as pressure, pain, and temporary hearing loss. That is to say, the sound is obstructed due to swelling.

Just as there are causes and effects of ear infections, if symptoms are ignored, there are causes and effects in our marriage when issues are not addressed. We can become infected with bitterness and unforgiveness. If we don't do anything, will they go away? Of course not. A seed will be planted, and the seed will continue to grow until it takes root. Once the seed takes root, more work has to be done to get rid of it.

So deal with the issues, they will not go away on their own! Just as there are warning signs before an ear infection surfaces, there are warning signs before the enemy of your marriage destroys it. You may feel that something is out of sorts and disconnected. However, the solution isn't to ignore the symptoms, but rather to address them. Remember the childhood game "Telephone?" The game went something like this: one person would start out by whispering a statement to another, and that person would tell another person what he/she thought was said. Each person would continue until the statement was told to the last person. The last person would tell what was said. Of course, what the last person stated would be totally different from what was whispered in the first person's ear. As often as we would play this game, I cannot remember a time that the first person's statement sounded anything like the statement from the last person. This was just a game, but this is the same game that the enemy is playing with marriages.

God is saying, "Your marriage shall not die but live," but the enemy of your marriage is saying, "Throw in the towel, it's not worth it." God is saying, "You can do all things through Christ who strengthens you." But the enemy of your marriage is saying, "You'll never become one." Whose report will you believe? I believe the report of the Lord.

Thought of the Week
Take care of your infection so you can hear clearly.

Prayer of the Week
Dear God, help us to hear You and not to believe the enemy as he whispers lies concerning our marriage. Help us to realize that we can become one in You. Help our love to always be for You, for one another, and for a lifetime. In Jesus' name, Amen.

Bridging The Gap

Reflections

Dana Fuller

Weeks 27-30
YOUR MARRIAGE TOOLBOX

Dana Fuller

Bridging The Gap

❦ WEEK 27 ❧

What's in Your Toolbox?

For his divine power has bestowed upon us all things that (are requisite and suited) to life and godliness, through the (full, personal) knowledge of Him who called us by and to His glory and excellence (virtue).
II Peter 1:3 (AMP)

Every home, no matter how big or small, needs a basic toolbox. Naturally, the toolbox by itself will not help fix the leaking faucet or hang a picture on the wall, but it will hold the tools you need to do the job and ensure the tools are right there when you need them. Without your toolbox, your tools will most likely end up scattered or even lost, all around your garage, basement, or maybe in the trunk of your car.

Think of Jesus as being your Master toolbox who houses all the tools you need in your marriage. In Him you will find every tool you will need to fix anything that is broken in your marriage, and without him your marriage would be scattered with no direction or purpose. You can easily go to Walmart and buy an entire 120-piece set made in China for $30. Fight the temptation. These inexpensive tools will not last a lifetime. If you have no clue about which brand to purchase, Craftsman tools are a pretty safe bet. They are durable and tough, and their hand tools come with a lifetime warranty. A lifetime warranty also comes with the words, "I do." Rome wasn't built in a day; neither are great toolboxes, and certainly not great marriages.

Some basic essential tools one may need in a toolbox are a hammer, measuring tape, an electric drill, pliers, and a screw driver, to name a few. You may not use every tool every day, but each will be used at one time or another. Some essential tools you will need in your marriage are communication, commitment, respect, trust, and forgiveness. A great place to learn about these tools are in relationship books. During the seasons that seemed as though my husband and I were disconnected, we both invested in books that helped us. Some relationship books that have been a blessing to us include:

- "Power of a Praying Wife" and "Power of a Praying Husband" (both by Stormie Omartian)
- "The Five Love Languages" by Gary Chapman
- "God's Little Devotional Book for Couples" by Honor Books
- "What Wives Wish Their Husbands Knew About Women" by James Dobson

My husband and I would read Honor Books' couple's devotional book together each night before bed. This was a great way to connect and spend time with one another. You and your spouse may decide to read it together each morning before starting your day. Do whichever works best with your schedule.

Thought of the Week
There is no greater power tool for building your marriage relationship than prayer.

Prayer of the Week
Dear God, thank You for equipping our marriage with every tool that we will need so that we may experience happily ever after in our marriage. Help our love to always be for You, for one another, and for a lifetime. In Jesus' name, Amen.

Bridging The Gap

Reflections

❦ WEEK 28 ❦

What's in Your Tool Box? (Communication)
Listen to advice and accept discipline,
and at the end you will be counted wise.
Proverb 19:20 (NIV)

Communication is a key factor in a successful marriage. When you are not communicating in your marriage, it is difficult to meet each other's needs. It took many years for my husband and I to understand this principle but thank God we did. We spent an incredible amount of time in the ring, talking about what was wrong with each other, playing the blame game—I'm right and you're wrong—rather than coming to the table with solutions.

Oh, we had both mastered the talking part of communication, but what about the listening? Once we began to listen to one another we could see subtle changes in the way we related. In a toolbox, you'll find that you will not use every tool every day, just as you would not use a wrench to hammer a nail. You must use the proper tool to assure the success of whatever you are repairing.

There are different types of communication tools: verbal, non-verbal, posture, facial expression, and the tone of voice. You may not use all of these at one particular time, and that's ok, but the key is to use them at some point when communicating to your spouse. My husband and I will be entering our 23rd year of marriage, and I consider us to be a well-seasoned couple in this area. However, even well-seasoned couples have communication breakdowns. As a matter of fact, we've just experienced this a few weeks ago. I was tired and I wanted my husband to pick up our son from basketball practice because he did not have to work this particular night. When he arrived home from work, he changed his clothes, put on his pajamas, ate dinner, and sat on the sofa. When he does this, I know automatically that he is in for the

Bridging The Gap

night. So when our son called the house and said that basketball practice was over my husband didn't budge, and I became upset, because I felt that I was just as tired as he was. I didn't express that I was bothered that he didn't volunteer to pick up our son, but how could he have known what I was feeling if I didn't communicate it to him?

I later looked at him and said, "You are not a mind-reader," and his response to me was, "What did I not do?" Your spouse doesn't have ESP. It's fine to give your spouse clues about what you need. Don't just assume that he or she knows what you are thinking; you must express how you are feeling in order to experience effective communication between you and your spouse.

Thought of the Week
Good listeners make good lovers.

Prayer of the Week
Dear God, just as Your ears are attentive to us, help us to be quick to hear, slow to speak, and slower to wrath in our marriage. Help our love to always be for You, one another, and for a lifetime. In Jesus' name, Amen.

Dana Fuller

Reflections

~ WEEK 29 ~

What's in Your Tool Box? (Love)
No one has greater love (no one has shown stronger affection) than to lay down (give up) his own life for his friends.
John 15:13 (AMP)

My husband and I, by far, are no experts when it comes to marriage, but we do have endurance underneath our belt when it comes to weathering the storms in our relationship. We've learned that maintaining a healthy marriage is much more than a puppy love or reading Harlequin romance novels. It's about the three loves defined from the Greek language that are essential to ensure the survival of a marriage experiencing happily-ever-after. As I mentioned in Week 13, they are: Agape, Phileo, and Eros.

Agape love is the greatest of them all—it's a self-sacrificing love. It moves people into action and looks out for the well-being of others, no matter the cost. Agape love is also an unconditional love—it takes a licking and keeps on ticking. It cares when there seems to be no reason to care, and it forgives when society says you should not forgive. Agape love is what God demonstrated toward us while we were yet sinners. Christ died for us (Romans 5-8). This love allows us to love our spouses regardless of their imperfections, or shortcomings. His love allows us to be patient and understanding. His love enables us to compromise when conflict arouses.

Phileo love is a friendship kind of love, a brotherly love. No matter how turbulent the storms have been in our marriage, my husband and I seemed to always maintain a level of friendship. Become a friend of the four C's: compassion, caring, consideration, and comfort. These four traits never grow old.

Eros love expresses sexual love or feelings. The Song of Solomon is a prime example of Eros love; the love between a husband and wife should be erotic; however, a long-term relationship based solely on erotic love will not last. You must incorporate the other two loves in your marriage until your marriage becomes seamless. A seamless marriage is one with no breaks or gaps; it is continuous without stopping. Columnist Ann Landers once wrote, "Love is an upper. It makes you look up. It causes you to think up. It causes you to be a better person than you were before." Love is an essential tool that is needed for you to experience happily ever after in your marriage.

Thought of the Week

The measure of a man is not how great his faith is but how great his love is.

Prayer of the Week

Dear God, help us to remember that love always protects, always trusts, always hopes, and always preserves. Help us create an oasis of love in our marriage that demonstrates a love that shall never be broken. Help our love to always be for You, for one another, and for a lifetime, in Jesus' name, Amen.

Bridging The Gap

Reflections

~ WEEK 30 ~

What's in Your Toolbox? (Forgiveness)

Therefore, as the elect of God, holy and beloved, put on tender mercies, kindness, humility, meekness, longsuffering: bearing with one another, and forgiving one another, if anyone has complaint against another; even as Christ forgave you, so you also must do.
Colossians 3:12,13 (NKJV)

We have all experienced hurt and disappointments in our marriage relationships and being able to forgive and release one's self of past hurts are essential tools for every marriage. Unforgiveness imprisons you both physically and emotionally, and can eventually lead to bitterness, and bitterness is linked to stress-related illnesses, such as: high blood pressure, strokes, ulcers, and heart attacks.

Just think, you have bleeding ulcers due to unforgiveness and the cure for these ulcers is to forgive. The ulcers would naturally heal itself but are we following the doctor's (God's) prescription? There are several scriptures that speak on forgiveness, but we're so focused on what he or she said or what he or she did, we ignore what the Word says. I'm not dismissing or diminishing the fact that you were hurt, but until you release past hurts, you will never be free, and your marriage will never reach its fullest potential.

So stop nursing your wounds with images of previous hurts that come into your mind. Stop allowing the enemy of your marriage to occupy space in your mind. One scripture instructs us to resist the devil and he will flee, but it doesn't say that he will not return **(James 4:7)**. I can guarantee that he will! Forgiveness means to wipe the slate clean, to pardon, and to cancel a debt. Jesus is a primary example of this principle: He died on the cross for all of our sins, past, present, and future, and He wiped the slate clean that we may have eternal life.

Wow! He did this just for us! We must be willing to do the same, to wipe the slate clean.

Thought of the Week
Lean on each other's strengths; forgive each other's weaknesses.

Prayer of the Week
Dear God, thank You for freeing and releasing us from past hurts, and disappointments. Just as You forgave us and continue to forgive us; help us to forgive and continue to forgive one another. Help our love to always be for You, for one another, and for a lifetime in Jesus' name, Amen.

Dana Fuller

Reflections

Bridging The Gap

Weeks 31-35
TEAMWORK

Dana Fuller

⋄ WEEK 31 ⋄

Fostering Teamwork in Your Marriage
The Lord God said, "It is not good for the man to be alone;
I will make a helper suitable for him."
Genesis 2:18 (NIV)

If you've ever played basketball, football, soccer, or any type of sports that require teamwork, I'm sure you are aware of the importance of playing *as* a team. We've all heard the saying, "There's no 'I' in the word 'team'." Although this is a true saying, my husband and I have had the opportunity to experience this first-hand. Our youngest son played in a basketball league called MSA. They practice once a week for about an hour, and their games are on Saturdays. At their first game it was quite obvious that they had created an 'I' in the word 'team'! The game was a wipeout. I believe the final score was 15-49.

Our son's team failed to understand the concept of teamwork. They had good, talented players on their team, but they didn't come together as a unit. They failed to have a successful game. You see, it doesn't matter how many super stars there are on a team; if the team doesn't work together as a cohesive unit, the result will always be the same.

During my son's second game, we could see more of a group effort from each team player. It was as if they had to see one another as a teammate and not an opponent. They learned one another's strengths and weaknesses and were able to use this to their advantage. This newfound knowledge was evident in the performance of their second game.

Teamwork in a marriage means you are working together for a lifetime—in good and bad times, in sickness and in health, and in adversity and prosperity. In order for a marriage to work, teamwork is an essential ingredient. Think about baking a cake from scratch. You can add the eggs, flour, butter, flavor, and baking soda; one ingredient on its own does not taste good, but all combined will make a delicious cake. In your marriage, on your own, you may be able to do wonders, but together you and your spouse can do the impossible.

Here are some key points to promote teamwork in your marriage:

- Encourage and support one another.
- Have open communication with one another.
- Have mutual respect for one another.
- Be dedicated and willing to act unselfishly.
- Be committed to the relationship.

In knowing your teammate, you can overcome difficult situations, gain confidence and trust in one another.

Thought of the Week
Your spouse is your teammate and not your opponent.

Prayer of the Week
Dear God, we acknowledge You as the Owner and Coach of our marriage. Thank You for teaching us practical principles that we can use to make our marriage thrive as a team. Help our love to always be for You, for one another, and for a lifetime in Jesus' name, Amen

Bridging The Gap

Reflections

∽ WEEK 32 ∾

Tune-Up Your Marriage

Practice what you have learned and received and heard and seen in me, and model your way of living on it and the God of peace (of untroubled, undisturbed well-being) will be with you.
Philippians 4:9 (AMP)

Have you ever driven down the road and all of a sudden, you look up at your dashboard and the check engine light is on? Now, this doesn't necessarily mean that there is anything major going on with your vehicle—chances are your car may just need a tune-up. A tune-up is an adjustment made to an engine in order to improve its performance. The maintenance on an automobile should be performed at an interval of 25,000 to 30,000 miles or two years, whichever comes first.

Some signs of needing a tune-up include knocking, surging, hesitating, smoking, and idling faster or slower than normal. So, if your check engine light is on, don't ignore it. Be a responsible driver and address the problem. Not making it a priority can result to severe damage to your car. Regular maintenance on your marriage is essential to establishing a strong, healthy, and happy marriage.

All marriages go through some bumps when left unattended, but a total breakdown can be avoided if you have a regular maintenance check-up your relationship. Remember the saying, "If it ain't broke, don't fix it?" Well, I'm here to tell you if you ignore potential warning signs that something is out of sorts in your marriage, you will experience some unwanted maintenance repairs that could have been avoided had you fixed what was broken. Make your marriage a priority by scheduling regular time to focus on just the two of you, so when challenging times arise you will be well prepared to handle them.

Bridging The Gap

We will sit for two to four hours while our car is being tuned-up, but we won't give our marriage the same consideration? If you want your marriage to be a marriage according to God's design, maybe it's time for a tune-up. You can start with thinking about your spouse's needs and desires. Leave little notes frequently in the car, the house, or your spouse's lunch box. Compromise is the key and understanding is the doorway to a successful marriage. Ask yourself, "What can I do for my marriage today, this week, this month, this year?"

Thought of the Week
A marriage may be made in heaven, but the maintenance must be done on earth.

Prayer of the Week
Dear God, help us to cultivate our marriage that it may grow and excel into a marriage according to Your master design. Help our love to always be for You, for one another, and for a lifetime, in Jesus' name, Amen.

Dana Fuller

Reflections

WEEK 33

Your Spouse is a Gift
Every good gift and every perfect gift is from above.
James 1:17a (KJV)

Remember the excitement you felt as a child coming up to the Christmas holidays? Your heart raced with anticipation upon seeing the wrapped presents under the tree. You would shake the boxes saying, "Wow, I wonder what's in here! Could this be the doll I asked for?" But no matter how often you may have shaken the boxes, it was not until you unwrapped the gifts that you knew what was inside. So often, I was surprised.

The Lord placed it in my spirit many years ago for my husband and I to host an annual couples' Christmas dinner. During the course of the night we would play several games that encouraged couples to work together and sharpen their communication skills. Some of the games played were bingo, gift exchange, and Let's Share A Drink. For the bingo game, we personalized the cards with words we tend to forget in our marriages such as communication, friendship, patience, romance, etc.

Last year, God blessed us to have yet another successful couples' Christmas dinner where we played games as well. One that stood out the most to me was the Gift Exchange Game. My husband and I placed gift bags under a Christmas tree that contained items the couples could use for a date night or just for spending time with one another. For example, one gift bag contained items for an indoor picnic: table cloth, chips, water bottles, and a gift card to Subway. Another example is a gift bag that contained materials for a baking night: a box of brownie mix, candles, and a CD with soft music. Each couple picked a number from a container, the couple with the number one chose a bag and opened it. The couple with the number two had the opportunity to either take the gift bag that couple number one had chosen or select a different bag. This continued until all couples had the opportunity to select a bag.

Although each bag contained gifts, they were all different. Each couple had the opportunity to take a gift bag that was more appealing to them. We so often look at other marriages and see something that we feel is more appealing and want it for our marriage. Just as there was something different in each bag, every marriage is different. It is good to emulate what we perceive is as a good marriage but remember that everything in another person's marriage may not be good for your marriage.

Your spouse is a gift and contained in your spouse are many differences. Appreciate the gift that you have and don't focus on the gift of another. Appreciate your gift and you will be surprised at what you will find.

Thought of the Week
You will never know the value of a gift until it's opened.

Prayer of the Week
Dear God, thank You for giving me my spouse. Thank You for giving me a gift that I can appreciate. Help me to love my spouse as You love me, unconditionally. Help our love to always be for You, for one another, and for a lifetime, in Jesus' name, Amen.

Bridging The Gap

Reflections

Dana Fuller

∞ WEEK 34 ∞

Insulating Your Marriage
So ought men to love their wives as their own bodies.
He that loveth his wife loveth himself.
Ephesians 5:28 (KJV)

I remember our first home just like it was yesterday. It was a three-bedroom, two-bath, split bedroom plan with a living room, family room, a formal dining room, screen porch, two-car garage located on a corner lot. Once closing was completed, we hired a contractor to do minor repairs on the roof, and a paint contractor to paint the entire interior of the house. My husband had a few friends assist him with laying ceramic tile down in the breakfast, kitchen, foyer, and bathroom areas. Once these tasks were completed, we moved in. The house was about 1,500 square feet, quite average for one's first home. It was built in 1983, but the foundation was solid and strong. The insulation, however, was a different story. Because the house was improperly insulated, our electric bill was often around the two-hundred-dollar mark in the summer and winter months, which was ridiculous for a home this size!

Insulation provides the walls of a house an effective layer of protection against excessive heat transfer, which results in proper overall thermal balance in one's home. It lowers the electric bill and deters house pests and insects. Just as insulation works to block the transfer of heat, keeping your home either cool or warm, so does God provide the insulation to your marriage. But He must be at the center of your marriage in order for your marriage to have the proper balance. Both husband and wife must listen to directions from God on how to treat, respect, and love one another. If both husband and wife listen to the instructions that the master planner provides, their marriage will be insulated from any pests and cold that may come against their union.

Thought of the Week
Proper insulation for our marriage comes from God.

Prayer of the Week
Dear God, thank You for insulating our marriage with everything we need in order for it to be according to Your master plan. Help our love to always be for You, for one another, and for a lifetime, in Jesus' name, Amen.

Dana Fuller

Reflections

~§ WEEK 35 &~

A Total Workout

And try to learn (in your experience) what is pleasing to the Lord
(let your lives be constant proofs of what is most acceptable to Him.)
Ephesians 5:10 (AMP)

Have you ever known anyone who has made exercise an integral part of their lifestyle? When they lay down, they think about what areas of their body to focus on or target the next day. Immediately after the alarm clock goes off each morning, they are off to the gym for an hour workout before work, and after work they are back at the gym for another regimented work-out.

A few years ago, my husband and I met a man in his early forties who was very disciplined regarding health and nutrition. For him, it wasn't just about working out, but also about eating the proper foods, drinking plenty of water and energy drinks. He was extremely selective about what he allowed to enter into his body. While vacationing, he visited us, and he and my husband went to the exercise room located in our community clubhouse. My husband said that he ran on the treadmill for about thirty minutes and from there he went to the pull up bars, then to the five-station workout area and back and forth from the various workout stations.

Wow! Talking about discipline! This gentleman envisioned what he needed to do to keep his body toned and knew the exact equipment to use to achieve his goal. This could not have been accomplished had he pushed the snooze button continuously every time the alarm clock went off. Snoozing will do absolutely nothing—you must do the work. No pain, no gain!

Think about where you are in your marriage and where you desire to be. Can you achieve these changes in your marriage by just thinking about them? Of course not! I remember when my best friend and her husband received premarital counseling before they were married and one of the questions that the pastor asked them was, "Do you think your marriage is going to work?" Their response was a resounding, "Yes, we do!" He proceeded to say, "Marriage doesn't just work, but you have to make it work."

Those unwanted pounds won't just disappear just by reading a book on weight loss; you have to change your diet and exercise if you want to have a toned body. Your marriage isn't any different. You can read every book in LifeWay, Family Life, and Barnes & Nobles on marriage and relationships; but it's not until you apply that knowledge will you receive the desired results. Then and only then you will begin to see your marriage transform into a marriage according to God's design. A marriage according to God's design is depicted as a triangle where God is at the top. Genesis 2:18 says, "It is not good for man to be alone." (NIV) God created woman to be a companion to the man. Each must depend on God. The closer they become to God the closer they will become to each other. Each exemplifies the attributes of God through forgiveness and love on their journey through life. In the midst of changes, they will model God's relationship between Him and His church.

Thought of the Week
How to be a happily married couple can never just be a thought, it must be learned.

Prayer of the Week
Dear God, thank You for giving us all of the equipment needed to have a healthy marriage. Thank You for the love, joy, peace, and respect that You have provided for our marriage. Help us to always use the equipment that You have provided. Help our love to always be for You, for one another, and for a lifetime, in Jesus' name, Amen.

Reflections

Dana Fuller

Bridging The Gap

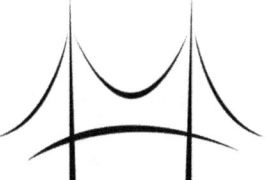

Weeks 36-39
LOVE

Dana Fuller

✧ WEEK 36 ✧

Romance in a Marriage

I will betroth you to me forever; yes, I will betroth,
you to me in righteousness and justice, in steadfast love, and in mercy.
Hosea 2:19 (NIV)

How would you define romance? Romance can be many things: it is how you express love and affection to one another. It is in a touch, or the way you look at your spouse. It's the language of love, and it is extremely vital to the success of your marriage relationship. We think affection is sex, but it's a small part.

I remember a time when the romance flames seemed to have evaporated out of our marriage. The word 'evaporate' has two senses: It's the process of becoming vapor, and the process of extracting moisture. The latter sense is what the romance in our marriage had become.

Before we knew it, the romance flames had been extinguished due to the hustle and bustle of life, church, children, work, and let's not forget, domestic duties of cooking, cleaning, doing laundry, and helping with homework. We had to realize that it takes work to keep romance alive in our marriage. It was up to us to make time for romance in our relationship, so we started doing the things that we did in the early stages of our courtship. Whenever we were in the car together, we would reach for one another's hand. When we were out on a date, we sat side-by-side. We left love notes in each other's car, in lunch boxes, even on the bathroom tissue. Small yet tender gestures take little time and effort but keeps us connected.

My husband and I recently started exercising together before work each morning and let me tell you there is something sexy about watching him pump iron with sweat streaming down his body. It is truly electrifying. Let me also say that it is important for our children to see us express our love for one another and to keep our marriage as a high priority. What we model before them regarding our marriage will have a great impact on their relationship with their future spouses. Remember that romance isn't just for anniversaries, birthdays, or Valentine's Day. Romance is for every day.

Thought of the Week
A successful marriage requires falling in love many times, always with the same person.

Prayer of the Week
Dear God, help us to rekindle the flames of romance in our marriage, help us to feed our marriage with love, attention, and appreciation for one another. Help our love to always be for You, for one another, and for a lifetime, in Jesus' name, Amen.

Bridging The Gap

Reflections

WEEK 37

Keeping Your Love Alive
*So guard yourself in your spirit and
do not break faith with your wife (husband) of your Youth.
I hate divorce says the Lord God of Israel.
Malachi 2:15b -16a (NIV)*

Falling in love is easy but keeping the flame burning is where we seem to fall short. Have you asked yourself these questions since you said, "I do":

"What happened to the passion?"
"Where has the love gone?"
"Have we just fallen out of love?"

All the love you thought you had for one another seems to have evaporated. In an earlier devotion, we talked about three of the Greek love languages: Eros love (sexual love or desire), Phileo love (a friendship love arriving from close association), and Agape love (the love God has for man and the love mankind has for God and other humans).

I do believe that if your primary focus in a relationship is based on Eros love, your relationship will experience a downward spiral. When the cares of life come, and trust me they will come, it will take more than an infatuation to get you through. Chauncy's and my relationship is one that exhibits all three of the Greek love languages mentioned above. We are not only lovers, but we are also friends, and because of Agape love we have been able to continue to love one another in spite of any storms that we have had to weather throughout our marriage.

Just remember, one of the most important principles to staying married is to do the things you did from the beginning. If you once gave compliments to one another and stopped, start back. Don't just think about the things that you admire about your spouse but express them. Pull out those love letters, blow off the dust and read them. Reminisce about how much in love you and your spouse were when you were dating and first married.

Thought of the Week
Where you are going in your marriage is more important than where you've been in your marriage.

Prayer of the Week
Dear God, we thank You for the covenant that we made to You. We vow to stay committed to You and one another. Help our love to always be for You, for one another, and for a lifetime, in Jesus' name, Amen.

Dana Fuller

Reflections

Bridging The Gap

❧ WEEK 38 ☙

Make Every Day Valentine's Day!
Let him kiss me with the kisses of his mouth:
for thy love is better than wine.
Song of Solomon 1:1 (KJV)

Valentine's Day is celebrated one day of the year, February 14th. It is a special day for couples to express their love and deep devotion to each other. During the celebration, it is common to see teddy bears, roses, flowers, and chocolate everywhere. It's nice to have a holiday to let our loved ones know we care about them, but don't just stop there. Let every day be an opportunity to show your love.

I remember on numerous occasions when my husband would call and say, "Don't make any plans for tonight.' He wanted to take me to dinner or to the movies. What made these times special were that they were not on a Valentine's Day. It's not about who can spend the most money on each other, but it's about appreciating and loving one another daily.

We would like to share an idea that we have used not just on Valentine's day, but on other days:

Love Retreat: Transform your bedroom into a private oasis where you can escape the outside world for a night. Purchase three dozen of red and white balloons and release them into your bedroom. Place red candles all around the room. Set a small round table and two chairs (a wrought iron patio table works great), lay out the attire that you desire your spouse to wear for the night along with the fragrance that he/she is to wear. Serve a three-course meal and feed each other side by side. We enjoy seafood, so I serve: fried shrimp, lobster, snow crab legs, and salad. To top it off, serve strawberry cheesecake. After dinner, soak in a tub filled with rose petals and give your spouse a massage. Then, lights out, camera, and action!

Thought of the Week
Marriage is like a marathon. It requires endurance.

Prayer of the Week
Dear God, thank You that we have an oasis of love in our relationship. Help us to cherish, love, and enjoy one another every day and not just on one special day. Help our love to always be for You, for one another, and for a lifetime, in Jesus' name, Amen.

Bridging The Gap

Reflections

WEEK 39

The Perfect Marriage
*Be completely humble and gentle;
be patient, bearing with one another in love.
Ephesians 4:2 (NIV)*

My husband and I recently started watching a television show called "My Fair Wedding," starring David Tutera, a celebrity wedding planner and bridal fashion designer. David meets the happy couple three weeks before their wedding day, and ultimately changes the entire wedding from the bride's dress to the location of the wedding. One of his sayings is, "Every bride has a vision, and I have revisions." His primary goal is to transform the wedding from less-than-ordinary to extraordinary. He becomes a personal guide to planning the perfect wedding, and he accomplishes this every time.

The wedding ceremony, however, is just that—a ceremony. Family, friends, and loved ones attend to witness one of the most memorable events in a person's life. The bride desires everything to be nothing less than perfect. Once the ceremony is over though and you've returned from the honeymoon, and unwrapped all the gifts, then marriage actually begins. What is a perfect marriage? A perfect marriage for a man could be dinner waiting on the table as soon as he walks through the door, not having to do any household duties, and having a guy's night out every night of the week. A perfect marriage for a woman could be shopping with no restrictions, never having to cook, clean, or do laundry.

We all may have various definitions of what we think a perfect marriage is. Some may even say there is no such a thing as a perfect marriage. I believe that the perfect marriage begins and ends with you. It has nothing to do with being perfect people. It's learning to compromise, support one another's dreams, aspirations, and desires.

It also is being able to make sacrifices, and if there is no sacrifice there is no love. John 3:16 says, *"For God so loved the world that he gave his only begotten son, that whosoever believeth in him shall not perish but have everlasting life."* (KJV)

Ask yourself, "What am I giving in my marriage?" Think about your spouse's needs and desires over your own. If each spouse commits to thinking of their spouse's needs and desires over their own, their relationship will grow. We do a lot of things to establish a relationship, but we don't do anything to keep it. As one plants a flower, one must continue to fertilize and cultivate it in order for it to bloom and grow. The process is the same for marriage if you want it to be all that it is designed to be. We must continue to cultivate our relationship.

Thought of the Week
The perfect marriage begins and ends with you.

Prayer of the Week
Dear God, help us to realize that a perfect marriage is not about us being perfect, but about us being selfless. Help us to focus on our spouse's needs and desires and not our own. Help our love to always be for You, for one another, and for a lifetime, in Jesus' name, Amen.

Dana Fuller

Reflections

Weeks 40-43
OVERCOMING TEMPTATION

Dana Fuller

Bridging The Gap

✥ WEEK 40 ✥

Fighting Temptation

*Watch and pray, that ye enter not into temptation:
the spirit indeed [is] willing, but the flesh [is] weak.
Matthew: 26:41 (KJV)*

Have you ever gone window shopping just to get out of the house, passed a window display and stopped completely in your tracks because of what was displayed on the mannequin? Then you proceed into the store to check out the price tag, and your mouth drops to the floor. The articles of clothing are totally out of your price range, so you turn and walk out of the store feeling disappointed. You try to get this out of your mind, but nothing works. About a week later, you find yourself back at the same department store gazing at what you were initially tempted by. You are so tempted to purchase everything on the mannequin fully aware of what's in your account.

Have you ever heard the saying, "Out of sight, out of mind?" Well, you can't get this particular display out of sight or out of mind. Temptation is getting the best of you, so, what do you do? Do you purchase the items using money allocated for other household expenses? Or do you resist the temptation?

We are all tempted at one time or another and there are various kinds of temptation. One may be tempted by food to eat excessively, another may be tempted to be a compulsive shopper, and another may be tempted to act on sexual fantasies with someone other than their spouse. Temptation in itself is not a sin but acting on the temptation is, and the repercussions can be detrimental. You can compare it to the after-effects of a hurricane: once it is over, there are still costs one must face. Will the home owner insurance cover the full cost of your home repairs, or will the funds deplete before the claim adjuster comes to access damages to your property? So, before you surrender to temptation ask yourself, is it worth it? Is it worth losing your spouse, children, and loved ones?

What's so amazing about temptation is it doesn't discriminate. It's not about color, sex, or age, but whoever yields to it. Temptation is real, and it has no respect of person. I'm not saying that thoughts won't come into your mind, but it's what you do with the thoughts. The Word of God says, it's not what goes into a man that defiles him, but it's what comes out. So when thoughts enter into one's eyes or ears that are totally against the will of God, remember that if we resist the devil, he will flee.

Thought of the Week
Temptation lies first in what you see and what you hear.

Prayer of the Week
Dear God, Your Word tells us that we will not be tempted beyond what we are able to bear. We ask for Your strength to stand under temptation. Help our love always to be for You, for one another, and for a lifetime, in Jesus' name, Amen.

Bridging The Gap

Reflections

Dana Fuller

∽ WEEK 41 ∾

Temptation 101

Therefore let him who thinks he stands take heed lest he fall. No temptation has overtaken you except such as is common to man; but God is faithful, who will not allow you to be tempted beyond what you are able, but with the temptation will also make the way of escape, that you may be able to bear it.
1 Corinthians 10:12, 13 (KJV)

Temptation has been around from the beginning of time. Remember the story of Adam and Eve in the Garden of Eden? God gave Adam specific instructions concerning what tree he could eat from. He was forbidden from eating from the tree of "Knowledge of good and evil." Yet, eventually, he does. God is on our side; He wants us to be victorious over every struggle and temptation, whether it is of God or Satan. As I stated in the last devotion, temptation is guaranteed to happen. It doesn't discriminate of age, gender, or race.

Certain things that we purchase in life may come with a lifetime guarantee. This means as long you live, the guarantee is extended to you. Well, temptation is the same way. Be assured that as long as you live, temptation will knock at your door, but it's up to you if the door opens. It comes in all fashions, whether it's lust or substance abuse, the end result is the same if you succumb to it. Let me say for the record, the enemy of your marriage will never tempt you in areas that you are strong in, but he will target areas that you struggle in. If your spouse isn't meeting your needs emotionally, there may be someone on your job who seems to listen and understand you more than your spouse does. That person actually connects with you. Remember, it is a trap, don't yield.

The enemy will entice you where you are most vulnerable, but you will never overcome temptation on your own strength. Philippians 4:13 says, *"I can do all things through CHRIST which strengtheneth me."* (KJV)

Bridging The Gap

It is through application of the Word that we will be able to overcome temptation when it comes. When Jesus was led by the spirit into the wilderness to be tempted, His escape was through the Word of God. Jesus always answered Satan with, "It is written." We must do the same. When Satan presents temptation in any form, we must remind him of what the Word says.

Think about a trap set for a mouse using cheese. The mouse is drawn to the cheese, but the sole purpose is to trap and kill the mouse. This is exactly what the devil does; he sets traps for us to deceive and destroy us. His ultimate goal is to place a gulf between us and our Maker. If he accomplishes this, he removes us from our source of power. But don't believe the lies of the enemy. He deceived Adam and Eve in the garden with his lies and his tactics aren't any different in the 21st century. He is still the author of all lies. So when temptation comes knocking at your door—and it will—remember what the devil intends as temptation, God allows as testing. What the devil intends as destruction, God allows as construction.

Thought of the Week
Every moment of resisting temptation is a victory.

Prayer of the Week
Heavenly Father, help us to remember in every temptation that we may encounter, You have provided an escape. Help us to always hide Your Word in our hearts that we may not sin against You. Help our love to always be for You, for one another, and for a lifetime, in Jesus' name, Amen.

Dana Fuller

Reflections

Bridging The Gap

⚜ WEEK 42 ⚜

Overcoming Temptation

*No temptation has seized you except what is common to man.
And God is faithful; he will not let you be tempted beyond what you can bear.
But when you are tempted, he will also provide a way out
so that you can stand up under it.
1 Corinthians 10:13 (NIV)*

Temptation is real, and we've all been tempted to act upon something that is against the nature of God. You may be tempted to keep extra change that was given to you by a cashier. You may be tempted to leave work early and falsify your time card, or you may be tempted to falsify tax return documents in order to receive a larger refund. I'm only listing a few, but the list can go on and on.

When my husband and I were first married, our finances were in disarray. Have you heard the saying, "Robbing Peter to pay Paul?" Well, we couldn't pay Peter and were having trouble paying Paul. We were living from paycheck to paycheck, just barely making ends meet. At this time, we banked with Suncoast Schools Federal Credit Union. One day I went to the credit union to deposit a three-hundred-and-thirty-dollar check. I completed the deposit slip requesting thirty dollars back in cash. Well, to my surprise when the bank teller returned the cash and the deposit slip, I proceeded to count the cash. The bank teller had given me three hundred dollars and had deposited the thirty dollars. I immediately glanced at the deposit slip and it was correct, however she had mistakenly given me the wrong about of cash back. Once I realized what had happened, I thought, "Oh the bills that my husband and I could pay with this extra money." Yes, that was my first thought, for those of you who have never been tempted. I guess you can say I was trying to justify a reason for me to keep the money. I remember thinking, "God, is this your way of bringing increase to us? It was her mistake, not mine, to receive Your blessing." But as I said in last week's devotion, temptation is not a sin, but it's acting upon the temptation that is a sin. I pushed the call button, explained to the bank teller what had just transpired, and she thanked me over and over again for giving the money back.

So, how do you overcome temptation when it comes knocking at your door? Recognize what tempts you, read the Word of God, and resist. Be honest with yourself and with God, and then read the Word of God daily. In doing so, you are getting the Word in your heart. Psalms 119:11 says, *"Thy word have I hid in my heart that I may not sin against you."* (NKJV) Renew your mind by meditating on the Word of God daily. If you renew your mind and don't feed your struggles, then you will be able to resist temptations when they arise. By the same token, if you do not renew your mind by meditating on the Word of God, when temptation arises you will yield. You must fight your temptations with the Word of God. Through application of God's Word, we can resist every temptation that we may come face to face with.

Thought of the Week
Remember, temptation is not a sin. We sin when we give in to temptation.

Prayer of the Week
Dear God, when temptation begins to brew in my thoughts, help me to recognize it, read Your Word, and resist every thought. Help our love to always be for You, for one another, and for a lifetime, in Jesus' name, Amen.

Bridging The Gap

Reflections

✥ WEEK 43 ✥

Defining Temptation
Watch and pray that you will not fall into temptation.
The Spirit is willing, but the body is weak.
Matthew 26:41 (NIV)

Temptation—how would you define it? It is when something makes you want to do something that you believe or know is wrong. Ultimately, temptation is designed to separate you from your Maker. The talented Michael J. Fox starred in the movie, "The Secret of My Success." He became successful due to determination, perseverance, and endurance. So what's the secret to overcoming temptation? Knowing the scriptures is good, but that is not enough. We must also meditate on them so when temptation comes knocking, we will be able to resist. Meditation is reviewing, repeating, and reflecting on the Word of God. Here are some helpful scriptures to meditate on when you become face to face with temptation.

> *Be self-controlled and alert. Your enemy the devil prowls around like a roaring lion looking for someone to devour. 1 Peter 5:8 (NIV)*

> *So I say, live by the Spirit, and you will not gratify the desires of the sinful nature. Galatians 5:16 (NIV)*

> *No temptation has seized you except what is common to man. And God is faithful; he will not let you be tempted beyond what you can bear. But when you are tempted, he will also provide a way out that you can stand up under it. 1 Corinthians 10:13 (NIV)*

> *Anyone who meets a testing challenge head-on and manages to stick it out is mighty fortunate. For such persons loyally in love with God, the reward is life and more life. James 1:12 (MSG)*

Bridging The Gap

For we do not have a high priest who is unable to sympathize with our weaknesses, but we have one who has been tempted in every way, just as we are yet without sin. Hebrews 4:15 (NIV)

Thought of the Week
Good habits result from resisting temptation.

Prayer of the Week
God of power, help me to resist temptation through meditation of Your Word. Help me to realize that in every temptation, You have made a way of escape. Help our love to always be for You, for one another, and for a lifetime in Jesus' name, Amen.

Dana Fuller

Reflections

Weeks 44-48
REVIEWING DR. CHAPMAN'S LOVE LANGUAGES

Dana Fuller

◆ WEEK 44 ◆

Love Language #1: Words of Affirmation
Death and life are in the power of the tongue:
and they that love it shall eat the fruit thereof.
Proverbs 18:21 (KJV)

There aren't any two individuals in the world who are exactly alike. Think about identical twins for a moment. They may look alike, dress alike, enjoy the same music, and share the same likes and dislikes and yes, they came from the same egg; yet in all their similarities, they **may still be different in other ways. Their personalities may differ, fingerprints, height, weight as well as their skin tone and textile and color of their hair.**

With the billions of people that make up the world we live in, we are all unique. We each have our own fingerprints, our own way of learning and understanding the world around us. What works best for one person, doesn't necessarily work for another. And just as we have different personalities, likes, dislikes, and learning styles; we all have different love languages. If you enjoy hearing your spouse, friend, or loved one tell you how special you are, and that the world is a better place because of you, your love language is "Words of Affirmation." This is the first one mentioned in Dr. Gary Chapman's book "The Five Love Languages."

To affirm means to strengthen, cheer on, and side with, supporting the value of your loved one. If this is your love language, then it's not the actions that cause your hearts to beat rapidly, but it's hearing, "Thanks for how you care for our children," or "That hair style is very becoming on you." Neglecting to speak this language to your spouse, no matter their love language, will result in your "love tank" becoming empty. Can you imagine driving your vehicle without any fuel? Once the tank is empty, all movement will cease.

Words of affirmation are powerful: They can either build up or tear down, give hope or discouragement, give life or death.

Thought of the Week
Words are a reflection of our thoughts.

Prayer of the Week
Dear God, help me to recognize my spouse's love language, and choose positive words that will build them up. Help our love to always be for You, for one another, and for a lifetime, in Jesus' name, Amen.

Bridging The Gap

Reflections

Dana Fuller

~ WEEK 45 ~

Love Language #2: Quality Time

To everything there is a season, and a time for every purpose under the heaven.
Ecclesiastes 3:1 (KJV)

Dr. Gary Chapman's book "The Five Love Languages" names "Quality Time" as the second emotional love language. If this is your love language, then you feel loved when you are spending time together with the one you love. Quality time is giving your spouse undivided attention with no interruptions from children, work, friends, telephone, or television.

Have you ever charted your course of a day? It might have gone something like this: Your alarm clock goes off around five. You dress in your workout clothes and head to the gym for a forty-five-minute workout. You shower at the gym so that you can arrive at work by 8:30am. You do your typical nine hours with an hour lunch break, punch the clock around 5:30pm, run a few errands before going home. You walk through your front door, have a little small talk during dinner, watch a little television, and then it's off to bed.

But small talk isn't enough. No matter how busy your day may get, spend at least fifteen to twenty minutes in daily dialogue with your spouse, without the TV or children. Spending time together communicates how much you care about your spouse and how much you enjoy spending time with him/her. Remember: It's not the quantity of time that is important, but the quality of time that counts. If you can spend nine hours of the day on your job and another hour at the gym, why couldn't you spend twenty minutes each day with your spouse, whether it's taking an evening walk together, washing the cars together, or pulling out and reading old love letters?

Bridging The Gap

Spending time with your spouse is one of the greatest gifts you can give. You will be amazed at how much your relationship will grow if you just spend time with one another.

Thought of the Week
If you don't schedule time for one another, you won't have time.

Prayer of the Week
Dear God, Your Word tells us that there is a time and a season for every purpose under the sun. Help us to realize how vital it is for our marriage that we spend quality time with each other. Help our love to always be for You, for one another, and for a lifetime, in Jesus' name, Amen.

Dana Fuller

Reflections

~ WEEK 46 ~

Love Language #3: Gifts
It is more blessed to give than it is to receive.
Acts 20:35b (NIV)

Gift-giving has been around for centuries. People give gifts for various reasons. Some do it out of guilt, some give them to be seen, and other give them as a symbol of their love to someone. Jesus demonstrated His love to us when He gave His life for us on the cross.

The one thing to remember about this love language is that it doesn't have to break your wallet or purse. Gifts are more than material things. They can be as simple as lending a listening ear or giving an apology or a hug. I find this language quite easy to relate to since this is one of my husband's love languages (along with Acts of Service). Everything in this zone comes easy for him. He gives freely.

For Mother's Day one year, I traveled to visit my Mom, and when I returned home, my husband had placed colorful streamers and party favors all around our family room, filled a basin with water, sat me in a chair and thanked me for caring for him and our boys. He and our boys proceeded to wash my feet. Afterwards, we made s'mores by the fire place. I felt like a queen! It's not about the size or the amount of a gift, but it is being able to give from the heart.

Let's remember to keep this in mind: when giving, give from the heart.

Thought of the Week
The value of a man resides in what he gives, not in what he is capable of receiving. Albert Einstein

Dana Fuller

Prayer of the Week

Heavenly Father, we realize that every good gift comes from You. Help us to be generous givers of our time, words, and money. Help our love to always be for You, for one another, and for a lifetime, in Jesus' name, Amen.

Bridging The Gap

Reflections

✥ WEEK 47 ✥

Love Language #4: Acts of Service

A generous person will prosper;
whoever refreshes others will be refreshed.
Proverbs 11:25 (NIV)

We all show love in different ways, and by the same token we all feel love in different ways. So what is your emotional love language? What ways do you tell your spouse that you love them? Remember the saying, "Action speaks louder than words." This is a true statement, especially if "Acts of Service" is your primary love language.

If an award were to be given for this love language, my husband would win by a landslide. It truly gives him pleasure to express his love to me through simple deeds, and of course I receive them with open arms. Let me clarify: If "Acts of Service" is your primary love language, whatever kind deeds you bestow upon your spouse aren't formed out of guilt, or sense of duty, but derived from the heart.

Almost immediately after my husband and I moved to our second apartment, our vacuum cleaner stopped working. The new one we purchased would leave a unique design in the carpet. My husband was very much aware of this so it gave him great joy to vacuum the carpet several times a week so that when I entered the apartment, I couldn't help but notice the design in the carpet. This may sound ridiculous, but it's true, and I'm grateful for such a small thoughtful gesture that would make my day every time. I'm sure some of you are thinking, "How can someone vacuuming the carpet, giving a foot massage, or leaving a note in a car saying, I love you, make one's day?" Well, those gestures can make one's day because these gestures simply said that my husband was thinking of me. Did he bestow these "Acts of Service" out of a sense of duty? No, he did them because it gave him great pleasure.

Bridging The Gap

Thought of the Week

Remember there is no such thing as a small act of kindness. Every act creates a ripple with no logical end. Scott Adams

Prayer of the Week

Dear God, help us to receive love to our spouse given in their love language. Help our love to always be for You, for one another, and for a lifetime in Jesus' name Amen.

Dana Fuller

Reflections

༺ WEEK 48 ༻

Love Language #5: Physical Touch

Place me like a seal over your heart, like a seal on your arm;
for love is as strong as death, its jealousy unyielding as the grave.
It burns like blazing fire, like a mighty flame.
Song of Solomon 8:6 (NIV)

The fifth and last love language that Dr. Gary Chapman discusses in his book, "The Five Love Languages" is "Physical Touch." I consider "Physical Touch" to be my primary love language. It's through this language that I feel most loved.

It's nothing for my husband and me to hold hands as we walk in the mall, a department store, or take a brisk walk in the park. I find that it's comforting to hold his hand as I drift off to sleep at the end of a busy and hectic day. Some may even think it's strange, but we also hold hands in church. It's something about my husband's touch, and I'm not just talking about the 'S' word (that's right, sex!). "Physical touch" can consist of holding hands, receiving a back massage, a hug or a kiss, and the list can go on and on. Sex is just one of the many aspects of the physical touch language.

For me, physical touch is extremely therapeutic. I often tell my husband that he missed his calling—he has some of the most soothing hands. At the end of the day, when the family has eaten dinner, the dishes are done and put away, my husband and I often sit on the sofa and watch television or converse about our day. He positions my legs on his and proceeds to massage my toes, legs, fingers, arms, and then my back. I can't tell you the numerous times that I have fallen asleep from receiving his kind, gentle, and loving touch.

Touch is a universal language, and even if this isn't your language, we all need to be touched at one time or another. Studies have shown that babies who have not been nurtured or touched have a greater tendency to exemplify destructive behavior that follows them throughout adulthood.

Now that we have given you small nuggets on each of the love languages discussed by Dr. Gary Chapman, I ask you: have you discovered your language? My prayer is that you have discovered not just your love language but your spouse's as well; and with this discovery you both will experience love for a lifetime. (You can take Dr. Chapman's love language quiz online at www.5lovelanguages.com.)

Thought of the Week
Sometimes it's better to put love into a hug than to put it into words.

Prayer of the Week
Heavenly Father, we pray that You will help us to keep our marriage emotionally healthy. Help us to realize although sex is part of "Physical Touch," a hug, a caress, or a gentle touch can speak volumes as well. Help our love to always be for You, for one another, and for a lifetime, in Jesus' name, Amen.

Bridging The Gap

Reflections

Dana Fuller

Bridging The Gap

Weeks 49-52
COMMON CHALLENGES

Dana Fuller

∽ WEEK 49 ∾

Premature Ejaculation
Trust in the Lord with all your heart
and do not lean on your own understanding.
In all your ways acknowledge him, and he will make straight your paths.
Proverb 3:5-6 (ESV)

Wow, what a topic! I'm sure some of you are saying, "Has she lost her mind?" My response to that question would be, "No, I'm just keeping it real." Yes, many years ago this topic was taboo, especially in the church arena. Times have changed though, and some churches are more apt to discuss the topics they seemed to avoid in times past.

Premature ejaculation (PE) is when a man ejaculates during sexual intercourse sooner than he or his spouse would like. It can be caused by stress over financial matters, depression, extreme emotional tension, or mere excitement. **Men, don't think that you are alone; studies** have shown that as many as one out of three men may be affected by PE at some time or another. PE can have a devastating effect on husbands and wives if it is not dealt with.

I believe the one key factor to overcoming this condition is effective communication. Communication is what helps us to connect with each other; it builds relationships, and allows us to express our ideas and emotions. What am I saying? You have to talk about it! Avoiding this topic can cause resentment, separation, and eventually the dissolution of your marriage. I am speaking from experience. I'm not an expert on this matter; however, life experiences can speak volumes.

I remember in the first stages of our marriage, my husband and I experienced this issue, and it wasn't until we addressed it that we were able to overcome it. We would begin with foreplay, and as soon as he would get started, it would be over. We would both say, "It's ok," but in our hearts, we both knew that it wasn't. I was left feeling frustrated, unfulfilled, and dissatisfied; he was left feeling embarrassed, frustrated, and ashamed. So, what do you do if this is you and your spouse? Well, some doctors recommend penis enlargement pills and creams. And these things may work. However, we chose a different route, which was the Word of God: "I can do all things through Christ who strengthens me." **Philippians 4:7 (KJV) Yes, even when it comes to our sexual life, we acknowledge Him.**

Proverbs tells us to recognize God in all of our ways and He will make straight our path (Proverbs 3:6) and that is exactly what we did. We acknowledged God and He made our path straight.

Now, Chauncy will speak on this topic from a man's perspective:

Premature ejaculation is a serious issue, one that many couples face but will not talk about. For a man, he may be able to get a release from the premature ejaculation, but it is not the same pleasure you experience when your wife is receiving her climax at the same time. It is frustrating and very embarrassing. At first, as my wife stated, we both said it was okay. We both were frustrated and bless her heart, she was patient as we went through that phase. And that's what it is, a phase. You don't have to stay there.

Men, you can try to think of different things while you are making love so you will not have a premature ejaculation. Foreplay should not be long at all. No matter how enjoyable it may be, you are setting yourself up for a disaster if you are in a phase of premature ejaculation and you try to engage in long foreplay. Be honest about it—tell your wife that you are embarrassed; she knows anyway.

Wives, be understanding and be sure not to blame your husband. Part of it is a mind thing and you definitely don't want your husband to start avoiding making love for fear of having a premature ejaculation. Continue to pray. Be patient, be kind, and be loving, because it is just a phase. Let me correct that statement, it should just be a phase. If it is not dealt with, it can last longer. So please deal with it.

Thought of the Week

Good communication skills are the key to good living.

Prayer of the Week

Father, we acknowledge You as Lord in marriage. Enable us to share our deepest thoughts and struggles with one another. Help our love to always be for You, for one another, for a lifetime, in Jesus' name, Amen.

Dana Fuller

Reflections

Bridging The Gap

∽ WEEK 50 ∾

Where Are The Fathers?
*As a father has compassion on his children,
so the LORD has compassion on those who fear him.
Psalm 103:13 (NIV)*

Remember the movie "Run Away Bride," starring Julia Roberts and Richard Gere? Julia Roberts played the role as a free-spirited young woman who was nervous and fearful about being married. She had left three grooms waiting at the altar on their wedding day. Richard Gere, a New York reporter was assigned to write a story about these events. In every relationship she encountered, the outcome was always the same: she would run.

This same attitude has plagued fathers throughout our society like wildflowers in the 21st century. As soon as a baby is conceived, oftentimes they are nowhere to be found. Research shows that more and more fathers are absent from their children's lives. An estimated 24.7 million children (36.5 percent) live absent from their biological fathers, and 26 percent of fathers live in different states from their children.

I firmly believe that if you were needed in the conception of a child, you will be needed in the raising of that child. Fathers are role models who teach their children to be strong adults. They model before their sons how a young man should respect his mom and women. A father also models before his daughter how a young woman should be treated by a man. A father ultimately models how to be the priest, provider, and protector of the home. Fathers, it is time to take back the responsibility of your home. It is not the mother's job to be the priest, provider, and protector of the home. God designed the father to take on this role. I'm not saying that a woman cannot do the best that she is able to do. I do realize in many cases the mother has to take on this responsibility in the absence of a father. I applaud the many women that have had to take on this responsibility, but it is not God's design. Fathers, take back your role and be the man who God has called you to be.

Thought of the Week
It is a wise father that knows his own child. William Shakespeare

Prayer of the Week
Heavenly Father, help our fathers to seek divine wisdom in order to receive direction to guide, instruct and encourage our children through life's journey. As parents, help our love to always be for You, for one another, and for a lifetime in Jesus name, Amen.

Bridging The Gap

Reflections

~ WEEK 51 ~

Oh, the In-Laws!
*Therefore a man shall leave his father and mother
and be joined to his wife; and they shall become one flesh.
Genesis 2:24 (NASB)*

Marriage is a beautiful institution designed by God, and when you say, "I do," remember, you are not only saying, "I do" to your spouse, but also to his/her family. My husband and I have been fortunate enough to have wonderful relationships with our in-laws, but I have heard enough horror stories from my co-workers and friends regarding their in-laws and family members so dramatic that one could produce a best-seller book.

Do your in-laws make you feel like your marital problems are your fault? Do your in-laws make you feel like you are not good enough for their son/daughter? Do they question your parenting skills, or undermine you in front of the children? No matter how difficult your in-laws may be, they are still your in-laws and, most importantly, they are still your spouse's parents.

So, how does one address meddling in-laws or other family members? I always like to go to the Word of God. What does God's Word say about in-laws? After God created Eve, and she became Adam's wife, God said, *"Therefore, a man shall leave his father and mother and be joined to his wife and they shall become one flesh."* Genesis 2:24 (KJV)

God realized the importance of cutting the cord from parents and being glued to one another from the beginning of time. This is called setting boundaries. You and your spouse must establish reasonable boundaries with your in-laws and other family members in case problems occur. How much, if anything, do you share with other family members? Should you loan money to family members or would you borrow money from other family members? These are questions, along with many others, that should be discussed during premarital counseling, to ensure that your marriage will soar as God has designed.

Thought of the Week
Setting up your own household doesn't mean you must terminate the relationship with your parents. Ed Young

Prayer of the Week
Heavenly Father, help us to strive to get along with our in-laws, realizing that they are family now that we are married. Help us to establish reasonable boundaries with our in-laws and family members. Help our love to always be for You, for one another, and for a lifetime in Jesus' name, Amen.

Dana Fuller

Reflections

Bridging The Gap

❧ WEEK 52 ☙

Empty Nest Syndrome
*Behold, children are a heritage from the Lord,
the fruit of the womb a reward.
Psalm 127: 3 (AMP)*

Growing up, I vividly remember one of my friends whose parents were active in their children's lives. My friend's mom was involved in Girl Scouts and assisted her in selling cookies every year. My friend's sister was involved in ballet and hip-hop dance. She had rehearsals on Mondays, Wednesdays, and Fridays. My friend's brother was also involved in every sport one could imagine at the high school. A calendar was posted on their refrigerator listing all of the children's activities and their mom and dad supported them one hundred percent. Between transporting the children and their friends to basketball games, dance recitals and to weekend camping trips, one would think their lives were complete.

That is usually not the case. Many families suffer because parents become so involved in making sure they support every detail of their children's lives that they lose sight of one another. Throughout the children's elementary, middle, and high school years, many parents are at every event the children have. All of the parents' spare time revolves around supplying the needs of their children, while little do they know that in the process of wanting to be good parents, they have neglected one another. Now, when the children graduate from high school and go off to college, they end up getting divorced. Their reason for getting a divorce?

"We've drifted apart."

Actually, it wasn't that they drifted apart; they realized too late that it was their children who kept them together. There has been a steady increase in the number of divorces among couples married thirty years or more, especially in the month of October. That's right—two months after the children are off to college, couples realize there is no relationship between husband and wife. Now that the children are gone, they find themselves living with a stranger.

Yes, our children need our support; yes, they need us to be active in their education, but in being there for the children, we can't neglect our marriage in the process. If this is you, there is hope. You and your spouse can stop the cycle now! Rebuilding and reconnecting with your spouse may seem awkward at first, but not impossible.

When our boys were younger, we early on began to reminiscence about life in the newlywed years of our marriage. Making love all over the house as frequently as we desired, coming out of the shower with no towel, going out for midnight snacks, going on weekend getaways, and not having to get a sitter. We also thought about changing one of our bedrooms into an exercise room. The list goes on and on. Please don't get me wrong, we love our boys, but we also love our marriage. We love spending time with each other, holding hands, and taking walks.

We will always be parents even when our children become adults—whether they go off to college, get married, or just move out on their own. We looked forward to the day when we would have an empty nest. The nest is now empty of children but not empty of appreciation, love, and respect for one another. Yes, we miss our children, but we will spend our remaining years loving, enjoying, and spending time with one another. For a lifetime.

Thought of the Week
Children should not divide a couple's love; they should multiply it.

Prayer of the Week
Dear God, thank You for gracing us with wisdom to instruct, to guide, and to inspire our children through life's journey. We thank You that

Bridging The Gap

in guiding and supporting our children, we will not lose sight of one another. Please help our love to always be for You, for one another, and for a lifetime. In Jesus' name, Amen.

Dana Fuller

Reflections

A FINAL THOUGHT

As I end the devotions for this year, I hope that I have provided information to assist in making your love last for a lifetime and to experience love by God's design. Take care and remember the best is yet to come.

Good communication is a lifeline of health to a marriage.

> *Reckless words pierce like a sword, but the tongue of the wise brings healing. Proverbs 12:18 (NIV)*

Heavenly Father, help us to be willing to discover our spouse's love language in order to experience a greater level of intimacy. Help our love to always be for You, for one another, and for a lifetime, in Jesus' name, Amen.

Dana Fuller

Dana Fuller

ACKNOWLEDGEMENTS

To my husband Chauncy, Thank you for being my greatest encourager, and for believing in me when at times I didn't believe in myself. Thank you for pushing me to reach higher, dig deeper, and to never settle for less. Thank you for your patience and understanding throughout the process (journey) of this book coming into fruition. I am so grateful that I get to discover love with you for the rest of my life. Thank you to our sons, Shaun, and Devin, for always keeping me accountable regarding the progression of the book whether through phone calls, texts, or face to face conversations. Thank you to my sister, Lynn, and her husband, James Warren, for always being inspirational whenever I needed moral support. Thank you to my dearest, closest, and best friend, Angela Peterson, for always speaking the truth to me in love. Our friendship means more to me than you will ever know. Thank you, Ruth Griffin, our publisher for your unmeasurable, endless patience during this entire process. You are truly a jewel. And to all my family, friends, and loved ones, thank you for your feedback, your encouragement, thank you all for your push, kind words, that I received from each of you.

Dana Fuller

ABOUT THE AUTHOR

Dana Fuller was born and raised in Clearwater, Florida where she received Christ and the baptism of the Holy Spirit as a teenager. Even at an early age, she knew there was a requirement on her life to fulfill the work of The Lord. She is an anointed vessel of God and ministers a prophetic Word in a practical way to all whom the Master leads her. The heart of her testimony is praise and worship. For Dana, Psalm 34: 1 "I will bless the Lord at all times His praise shall continually be in my mouth" is more than inspiring it is her strength. It is that same spirit of might and spirit of wisdom that gives her the ability to teach the uncompromising Word of God with passion and conviction. Though content and diligent in the "ministry of helps", God has brought her to the forefront "to sound the alarm in His holy mountain" (Joel 2:1) to give mankind a wake-up call" in the area of marital relationships.

God has placed in Dana a desire to see "heaven's best in marriages." She knows it has always been the Father's will for husbands and wives to enjoy "a wholeness and fullness" in marriages…not missing out on anything God has for them. In Genesis 2:24b "…and they shall be one flesh", Dana has seen that the "shall be" is a process by which one must pray, read the Word of God, listen to the voice of the Spirit and WORK THE MARRIAGE! She knows you can't be so "prophetic" that you neglect the "practical" or so "spiritual" that you overlook the "simple".

Dana founded Love for a Lifetime Ministries with the purpose of practically teaching couples how to live and love in their marriage through the Word of God. Through the transparency of experiences in her own marriages, Dana's prayer is that a seed will be planted, it will take root and grow to bring forth "much fruit" in the marriages she encounters. She desires that husbands and wives will allow their love to be "For God, For one another, For a Lifetime."

Dana is a devoted wife of thirty-one years to Chauncy Fuller who lovingly supports her fully in the mission God has given her. She is also a dedicated mother to her two sons, Shaun, and Devin. She has a strong sense of family and believes the best way to manifest Christ to the world is to first fulfill her "call" as a wife and mother, to the glory of God.

www.ingramcontent.com/pod-product-compliance
Lightning Source LLC
Chambersburg PA
CBHW071436080526
44587CB00014B/1870